OPTIMISM
PRESS

The
Courage
of
Compassion

The
Courage
of
Compassion

A JOURNEY FROM JUDGMENT
TO CONNECTION

Robin Steinberg

AND CAMILO A. RAMIREZ

OPTIMISM PRESS

Optimism Press
An imprint of Penguin Random House LLC
penguinrandomhouse.com

Most Optimism Press books are available at a discount when purchased
in quantity for sales promotions or corporate use. Special editions, which
include personalized covers, excerpts, and corporate imprints, can be created
when purchased in large quantities. For more information, please call
(212) 572-2232 or email specialmarkets@penguinrandomhouse.com.
Your local bookstore can also assist with discounted bulk purchases using the
Penguin Random House corporate Business-to-Business program. For assistance
in locating a participating retailer, email B2B@penguinrandomhouse.com.

LIBRARY OF CONGRESS CATALOGING-IN-PUBLICATION DATA
Names: Steinberg, Robin, (J.D.), author. |
Ramirez, Camilo A., 1985– author.
Title: The courage of compassion : a journey from judgment
to connection / Robin Steinberg and Camilo A. Ramirez.
Description: New York : Optimism Press, an imprint of Penguin Random House
LLC, [2023] | Includes bibliographical references and index. |
Identifiers: LCCN 2022042749 (print) | LCCN 2022042750 (ebook) |
ISBN 9780593084625 (hardcover) | ISBN 9780593084632 (ebook)
Subjects: LCSH: Steinberg, Robin, (J.D.) | Public defenders—New York (State)—
New York—Biography. | Criminal justice, Administration of—United States.
Classification: LCC KF373.S6894 A3 2023 (print) | LCC KF373.S6894 (ebook) |
DDC 340.092 [B]—dc23/eng/20230106
LC record available at https://lccn.loc.gov/2022042749
LC ebook record available at https://lccn.loc.gov/2022042750

Printed in the United States of America
1st Printing

Book design by Chris Welch

Some names and identifying characteristics have been changed
to protect the privacy of the individuals involved.

To Our Children's Children's Children

The stories in this book are true. Everything from personal conversations to courtroom proceedings reflects my best, but surely imperfect, memories of the events.

CONTENTS

A Letter from Simon Sinek

I started Optimism Press to help advance a vision of the world that does not yet exist. A world in which the vast majority of people wake up every single morning inspired, feel safe wherever they are, and end the day fulfilled by the work that they do. The single best way for us to build this world is if we commit to building it together.

But there's a problem. . . .

We will be able to build that world only if we can truly listen to one another. But we don't. Instead, we speak at one another. We have reduced those with whom we disagree into caricatures that we can easily dismiss or even hate. We argue about things with a kind of rigid moral authority we don't have—both sides believing they are on the side of right and good, and seeing the other side as wrong or evil. And because we too often succumb to "us versus them," we become unable to see "the other side" in their full humanity, which hijacks any opportunity to foster genuine connection or dialogue.

That's where *The Courage of Compassion* comes in.

This is a book told through the lens of criminal justice, but it is not about criminal justice. The real story is about learning to see all people as human—complicated, messy humans—no matter what. Robin Steinberg directly challenges us to consider the question *What if your entire life were defined by the worst thing you ever did?* And if we don't want that for ourselves (and we have all said or done unethical or shameful things in our lives), then how can we do that to others? The answer, it turns out, is as complicated as the journey to get there. *The Courage of Compassion* is determined, however, to go on that journey with us.

You will read about cases of justice and injustice. Parts of this book will make you angry. Parts will make you sad. Parts will frustrate you. You will find yourself judging people you don't know, maybe even the author. And that's the point. This book pushes us to take ourselves on. It challenges us to replace our judgment with curiosity.

I chose to publish a book written by one of the pioneers of a controversial topic—criminal justice and bail reform—for the same reason I founded a nonprofit organization called the Curve Initiative, which works with police chiefs and sheriffs from across the country to help evolve the culture of policing from the inside out. Though these two groups are often pitted against each other, the truth is, many people on both sides share a very similar vision of the world, despite what appear to be intractable obstacles to change.

If we want to improve our institutions and make this world a better place, we have to be willing to learn to listen to and work with people with whom we don't agree and may not even like for one very simple reason—we cannot make peace only with our friends. If we are to find any common ground to benefit the greater good, we have to find ways to see those on "the other side" as human and extend a hand. If we want to live in a world in which we feel seen and heard and understood, we have to find a way to look beyond our differences and recognize how much we have in common. And the single best way to do that is to learn the courage of compassion.

Show compassion and inspire on!

Simon Sinek

AN INVITATION

Could you love someone who committed murder? I'm not talking about someone wrongfully accused or even someone with a legal justification for taking the life of another. I'm talking about someone who did it, pure and simple. Can you imagine yourself caring for them? Maybe more to the point, why would you want to?

For the past forty years, I have explored these questions. Not as a philosopher or an academic but as a lifelong public defender and social justice advocate. In my role as a public defender, I have defended people charged with things as insignificant as riding their bicycle on a public sidewalk and as significant as viciously shooting someone in the head for no apparent reason. With each client, and each story, I grappled with the moral, political, and real-life implications of defending someone charged with committing a crime as everyone around me asked the question: "How can you defend those people?"

There is no single answer. I'm not sure that, even after a long career in the trenches, I can fully answer the question. What I do know is that the system we have created to adjudicate right and wrong and determine criminal responsibility and punishment is deeply flawed. Over the past couple of years, there has been an awakening about the ways in which America's criminal justice system has perpetuated racism and injustice. People on both sides of the aisle are calling for change. However, does recognizing the need for change and even saying it out loud lead us down the path to real reform? Is the recognition alone enough to create the necessary change?

I wish it were that simple. Seeing the systemic flaws is a necessary first step to change, but it will not be enough. The truth is that we are a deeply punitive people. In the new court of public opinion, our desire for social and racial justice is bold and restorative, but in our courts of law, even amid today's movement for change, justice more closely resembles bloodthirst. What propels us to continue such cruelty? Why do we punish so unforgivingly? Why do we reduce people to their worst moment, rather than see them in the fullness of their humanity?

After many years of fighting from within the system, I have realized that a big part of the problem lies within each one of us. Our inability to recognize ourselves in "those people" and see our shared humanity is at the heart of our cruelty. It is that distance that has enabled our criminal justice system to operate for generations, crushing the people who become ensnared in it. So what will it take to transform our criminal justice system?

Nothing short of changing ourselves, one person at a time.

Let's be honest: we are all "criminals." Each one of us has done something that could be defined as criminal—driving home after a few too many drinks, taking an illegal drug, getting into an argument that turned physical, or being less than truthful on a tax return. These are all crimes. Some of us have been arrested; others of us have been lucky or privileged enough to evade prosecution. Whether or not our crimes have landed us in the criminal justice system or not, we are all flawed, and none of us wants to be defined by our most shameful moment. Indeed, the words "that's not who I am" have been uttered in equal quantity by those charged with burglary and those charged with crimes related to storming the Capitol on January 6.

Let me be clear: I am not suggesting that people shouldn't be held accountable for their crimes. We should all be held to account for the things we have done wrong and the harm they might have caused. That goes without saying. But what that looks like, and how we administer justice, must consider the context of an act and the humanity of the actor.

This book will take you into America's criminal justice system and into the lives and stories of some of the people caught in it—people whom I represented over the years and who taught me the most important lessons of my career. I hope that this proximity to them will open your eyes to how our system operates. But I hope you will go deeper, as I myself have done in this book by reflecting on my own personal story, my career as a public defender, and the experiences that shaped me. In sharing my path, I also hope you'll recognize some truths about yourself.

I am inviting you to go on a journey to face your own judgments, fears, and beliefs and to recognize how they might be reflected in our systems. This journey may be emotional. It will for sure make you frustrated at times. And it may even make some of you mad enough to stop reading. But one thing is for certain: this journey will take courage.

Robin Steinberg

1

How Can You Defend "Those People"?

Like every public defender, I have been asked this question countless times at parties, holiday meals, family gatherings, in the courtroom, and even on the street after a trial. People have also demanded an answer in hate mail, media interviews, and other less-than-friendly venues. My responses range from the flippant to the philosophical and purely political. The fundamental importance of the right to counsel. The primacy of the presumption of innocence. The need to check government power. Mass incarceration. Frankly, these answers are the autopilot reply for a career defender. And there is truth in them. But they do not fully explain why I chose to devote my life to defending people at the mercy of our criminal justice system, and to dedicate my-self to changing it.*

In America, anyone accused of a crime that carries with it a possible sentence of incarceration is entitled to counsel. This right to an attorney is a critical safeguard to protect those most vulnerable when the government seeks to take away liberty. Public defenders breathe life into that concept. They are the only in-stitutional actors in the criminal justice system with the sole and unequivocal responsibility of defending the accused, no matter what the charge.

The guarantee of a public defender for the poor is essential to the proper functioning of an adversarial system of justice and has become even more critical given our seemingly insatiable appetite for jailing people, even before they've had a trial.

Mass incarceration is a truly American phenomenon. While

---

* In recent years, many social justice organizations and advocates have started using the term *criminal legal system* rather than *criminal justice system* to de-scribe America's system of jails and prisons, criminal courts, prosecution, and policing. The argument is that the current system does not deliver justice. Thus, to call it so is inaccurate and corrupts the meaning of justice. Indeed, as we know all too well, the fact that something is legal does not make it just or right. I agree with the spirit of this argument. However, I have chosen to use the term *criminal justice system* throughout this book because the moral challenge, as I see it, is transforming what we mean and expect from justice in the first place. The truth is that Americans largely expect retribution in response to harm and wrongdoing when it comes to the administration of justice. Trading terms might evoke a sense of progress, but it does not funda-mentally challenge us to think differently or work toward a new definition of justice.

the term *mass incarceration* has finally made its way into popular culture, I'm not entirely sure most people understand how truly horrifying the scale of this problem is.

America is home to less than 5 percent of the world's population, but about 25 percent of the world's incarcerated people live in America.[1] Even by conservative estimates, at least five million people churn through our jails every year.[2] That is larger than the combined population of Phoenix and Chicago, *every year*. It is no surprise, then, that nearly one in two adults in the United States has had a family member incarcerated, and as many as one in three has some type of criminal record.[3] What's more, nearly two thirds of people in jail on any given night are not even serving sentences.[4] They are behind bars awaiting trial, mainly because they cannot afford cash bail. Our criminal justice system has become so massive, it is the largest employer in our nation . . . right after Walmart.[5] In fact, we run as many prisons, jails, and other correctional facilities as we do hospitals.[6]

These alarming figures make us the most incarcerated nation on earth, yet we are no safer than countries with far fewer jails and prisons relative to their populations. But that's not all. Mass incarceration intersects with and compounds another crisis in our country: systemic racism. I'm talking not about individual acts of racial bias, conscious or unconscious, but about the way in which our history has shaped policies, institutions, and social practices to produce disparate outcomes in nearly every aspect of Black Americans' lives, from health and education to criminal justice and economic opportunity. When it comes to our criminal justice system, this problem is evident at every stage of the process. Black Americans are not only more likely to be stopped by the police, searched, and subjected to excessive use of force; they are also more likely to be detained before trial, overcharged, and harshly sentenced.[7]

While I wish I could say it was purely my shock at our incarceration rates, or even the purity of the idea of a right to counsel, that drew me into public defense, there was also another influence: a group of women.

The year was 1980 and I was a law student at New York University School of Law. I had signed up for a law clinic called the Women's Prison Project, where law students worked under a supervising attorney to represent women on a variety of issues, including health care, child custody, and parole matters. The fact that the clinic served women in a maximum-security prison was largely incidental to me. I simply wanted to advocate for women wherever they were, and this was the only clinical offering that focused on women. Little did I know at the time that it would change my life.

Over the course of a year, I traveled to and from Bedford Hills Correctional Facility, oddly located in one of the most bucolic and affluent towns in New York, not far from Martha Stewart's 153-acre farmhouse estate. Each visit drew me closer to the women I interviewed for the project and the deeply personal stories they told me about their lives and their families.

They were nearly all Black women. They spoke about trying to overcome crushing poverty. They spoke about their children and their hopes and dreams for a better future. They spoke about feeling helpless in the face of a system that was merciless. Some swore by their innocence. Others explained there was more to their story than the crime they had committed. They also spoke about not feeling heard or understood by the very lawyers sworn to defend them. This surprised me. They explained their public defenders didn't spend enough time with them, listen carefully, or care much about them. Few could even name their attorney or the specific crime they were convicted of, but each could tell me exactly how many days, months, and years they had left to serve away from their children.

At night, in my tiny East Village apartment, I went over my notes from those visits and thought about each of them. It was on one of those nights that I decided to become a public defender. It was a simple realization. Other more patient souls could devote themselves to civil rights lawsuits, class action litigation, and policy reform. I, for one, could not think of anything but how to keep these women from being sent to these prisons in the first place. I wanted to stand by their side in those courtrooms, defend them, and push back against the system that would take them from their children, families, and communities. Listening to the women at Bedford Hills made me wonder: Who were these public defenders, and why did they fail these women so miserably? To find out, I joined my law school's criminal defense clinic.

On the morning of my very first court appearance, I changed clothes three times before leaving the house, settling on a gray suit, white blouse, and black pumps. Back then, for a woman, looking professional meant wearing the closest thing to a man's suit that you could find. I had a new black briefcase to carry my files, a spare pair of pantyhose, and my wallet with my identification. As I headed down the stairs of the subway station on Fourteenth Street to meet my clinical professor, I was filled with anticipation. I'm not sure what I was expecting, but I'm pretty sure my twentysomething-year-old self imagined she would be walking into movie-like, marble-columned courtrooms, where judges dispensed justice based on law and evidence and lawyers fiercely debated the merits of a case. As I would soon learn, nothing could have been further from the truth.

I will never forget the horror I felt when I set foot in Manhattan criminal court. The so-called war on drugs was in full swing, police departments were expanding, mandatory minimum sentences were all the rage, and the public made it clear that anyone who appeared "soft on crime" would pay the electoral price.

A corrections bus pulled up next to the building. One by one, people chained together stepped down and were led through a small door on the side of the courthouse, where they disappeared from sight.

Inside, the hallways were packed with families and children, most of them Black and Latino, waiting anxiously for the courtroom doors to swing open. Once they opened, a frenetic energy filled the air as family members poured into the dark courtrooms, each with enormous, filthy windows, flickering fluorescent lights overhead, and those famous New York City pigeons, which had somehow found their way onto the rafters. As court officers called out names, people in handcuffs walked into the courtroom, flanked by armed guards. Family members would strain to see their loved one. They would sneak a wave and share a smile. And there were tears, so many tears.

There were no brilliant legal arguments that day, no beautiful marble columns, and definitely no passionate lawyers debating the rights of their clients—or debating at all. Mostly, the judge discussed convenient court dates for the lawyers, barely noticing that there was a human being in handcuffs standing in front of them. It didn't take me long to realize that this was what passed for justice in America. We take the poorest and most vulnerable people in our society and put them in cages, expecting that somehow this is going to solve the larger issues that drive people into the system in the first place.

In America, we want to believe that our system is fair and balanced, but in practice our system is less a pursuit of justice and more an exercise in power and dealmaking where resources make all the difference. The burden of proof might be on the prosecution to prove guilt beyond reasonable doubt, but if you are poor, the odds are against you, starting with your inability to afford cash bail or get effective representation from an overworked and under-resourced public defender. There is no fair fight—it's a slaughter.

Witnessing this slaughter changed something in me. I couldn't just stand by. I realized that if I wanted to change things, I had to begin in the here and now with the things I could control. In my case, that meant approaching the representation I provided each and every client not just as a job but, on a more personal and human level, as the most important thing I could be doing at the moment.

One by one, those moments with my clients transformed my life in more ways than I could imagine. There is a unique intimacy between lawyer and client when public defenders live up to the responsibility of protecting another person's rights and dignity, if only by virtue of their inherent and inalienable humanity. Public defenders meet people at some of the lowest points in their lives, moments that strip them down to their basic human condition and when the stakes could not be higher. Before you there is a person whose entire life, worth, and character are being judged by prosecutors, judges, and society through the myopic lens of a single act. As a public defender you must push past that paradigm and replace judgment with curiosity.

It's not easy. In fact, we are naturally predisposed to judge—it has been the key to our survival. But judgment can also obscure.

Most people can imagine why a lawyer would defend someone who is innocent of an alleged crime, no matter how serious the accusation. But trying to explain why I would defend someone *who I know is actually guilty*, particularly of a violent crime, is usually met with scathing judgment, not just of the person I represent but of my own character.

"How can you do that?" "Don't you feel guilty?" "Isn't it immoral?" While I understand why those questions are posed, I never struggled with a moral quandary in this regard. That's not to say that I couldn't recognize when my clients' actions had caused real harm, trauma, or even death. Instead, what I reject is the idea that a person can ever be less than human—no matter what they've done. Even a person guilty of a crime should be treated with dignity.

Translating this insight into practice requires curiosity—a genuine curiosity about how a person arrived at the present moment and the forces and events that shaped their circumstances. We come into this world with wide-eyed curiosity about everyone and everything that we encounter. But by the time we reach adulthood, much of that spark has dimmed. To be a great public defender you must awaken your curiosity so that your mind is open to seeing the person standing next to you, in their entirety, as you fight for them. There is always a context, a history, an iceberg of experiences beneath what we see of another person. For me, every client was a marvelous puzzle, and the case file was only a piece of it.

In my life as a public defender, curiosity taught me that no one is wholly bad, or even wholly good. People can do bad things, of course, but that is the starting point of getting to know your client, not the endgame. My decades as a public defender confirmed the old adage that hurt people hurt people, calling into question the wisdom of a system that practices justice in the form of retribution. Scarlett Lewis, an author and advocate whose six-year-old son was killed during the tragedy at Sandy Hook Elementary School, summed it up this way: there are only two kinds of people in the world—good people and good people who are in pain.[8]

We must seek to imagine what it would be like to be in the other person's place and the journey that could have brought them there. Just for a moment, think about the worst thing you've ever done. Whatever you're most ashamed of. Keep it to yourself. Now ask yourself: Should your entire life and character be defined by it? If your answer is no, congratulations, you have passed the first test of becoming a public defender. You want others to see you as fully human, so you must learn to see others in that way. This is important not only because you yourself would not want to be defined by your own worst act but also because tapping into this capacity of our imagination for compassion enhances our sense of connection to others. We see how we are all the products of a context and so much more than the sum of our mistakes.

Everyone locked in a cage experiences some combination of fear, depression, anger, and anxiety. In that position, it takes courage to trust a stranger and share some of the most personal details about your life with them in the holding cell of a courthouse or a jail. But that's what people who are assigned counsel are forced to do—to place a tremendous amount of hope and trust in a complete stranger. In those moments of trust, I couldn't help but become devoted to the person in front of me. For when you open yourself up to the pain and suffering of another—when you step into his or her world even for a moment—you can't help but want to do something. It is not guilt, politics, or even alliance because of a common identity but a deep and unavoidable sense of shared humanity that compels action. It is the courage of compassion.

Every person I have represented since has reinforced my path, even the ones who made me question whether I had what it took. It is they—their lives, their stories—who have compelled me and inspired me to stay in this fight for as long as I have. For me, only people can do that. Not ideas, not theories. People. How can I defend "those people"? Easy. I choose to defend people. I do so because I believe we are all worthy of compassion. I also believe we are all capable of it.

We all think we are compassionate, just as we all think we are honest. But true compassion is not innate. Compassion for others, especially those whom we don't know or understand, must be learned. Being a public defender did not teach me compassion. Finding the courage to love an unlovable person did. So perhaps I should go back to the beginning.

2

Idealism versus Reality

I am the product of two people who had absolutely no business being married to each other, much less having children. They met while stopped at a red light at an intersection in my mother's hometown in Pennsylvania coal country.

My father, the story goes, took one look at my mother, jumped out of his convertible, leaving it abandoned in the street, and went over to my mother to introduce himself. She was a senior in high school; he was barely nineteen. She was used to dating the local star football player, sang in the school chorus, and was voted "girl most likely to succeed." He was handsome, charismatic in a James Dean kind of way, sarcastic, and troubled. He hated school, his parents, and anything that involved rules.

My father's impetuous and reckless abandonment of his car should have been a warning sign for my mother about what was to come, but she ignored all reason and gave him her number. It wasn't long before he showed up on the doorstep of my grandparents' home asking if he and my mother could go on a date. To say that they were from completely different backgrounds would be an understatement. Nothing about them as a couple made sense, except that they were passionately and irrefutably in love with each other. At least during those early years.

From the moment that my parents met on that sunny afternoon, in the middle of an intersection, their fates were tied. They looked right past their religious, class, and regional differences and saw only each other. My mother ignored all the warning signs that my father might be trouble, turning a blind eye to his arrests, substance use, and wild mood swings. Or perhaps it was precisely those things that drew her to him, combined with his tendency toward grand gestures.

On the night of her high school senior prom, as they exited the dance hall, my father said he had a surprise. He began to drive— past her high school, past her church, and past her house—until they were on the highway. He drove her ninety miles to his home turf, New York City, where he had reserved a table at the Blue Angel in Midtown Manhattan. Ella Fitzgerald was singing that night. I can only imagine how swept away my mother must have felt by my father and the world he was offering. But she had a 5:00 a.m. curfew, so right after the show they got back on the road and drove home to Pennsylvania, arriving a few minutes shy of

5:00 a.m., only to see my grandfather on the porch, watch in hand. It would not be long before she ran away to convert to Judaism so they could marry.

Years later, long after my parents' marriage had ended and my father had died, my grandfather told me that he knew from the first time he met my father that he was "trouble." But, he conceded, he also knew that no one was going to be able to stop them from being together.

My childhood was filled with uncertainty. We moved six times in the first seven years of my life, going from place to place as my father tried to find stable ground under his feet. His mood swings, impetuous behavior, and angry outbursts were softened only by his famous grand gestures and promises to change. As a child, I had a front-row view of it all. Barely adults themselves, they made no effort to shield me from their reality. My mother was focused on my father, above all else. So as my father descended into what would eventually be diagnosed as the dual challenges of bipolar disorder and a raging addiction to cocaine and heroin, I was left largely to fend for myself, and then for my baby brother, who came along seven years later.

I grew up with inauthentic authority. My parents may have had the status of authority figures by virtue of the fact that they were my parents, but the way they behaved commanded little to no respect. The unexpected by-product is that I have a healthy dose of mistrust for anyone in a position of power.

For me, that distrust showed itself at an early age. In elementary school, the teachers noted that I was too rebellious. Fair. By middle school, I had begun to question the entire construction of America's educational system, and by the time I was in high school, I had simply stopped attending class. No one seemed to notice.

As the years went by, my parents' marriage continued to deteriorate. My father would disappear often, sometimes for weeks, leaving my mother to fend for herself. During those times, she was so distraught that I took over most of the household chores and care of my brother. There were phone calls that came at all hours from the women my father was seeing. I would hear her yelling at them until she slammed the phone down. Then I would watch as she sat on the stool in the kitchen, smoking Salem menthol cigarettes, pack after pack, engulfed in smoke, sadness, fear, and helplessness. It was the helplessness that I hated more than anything, a helplessness I saw in so many of the women in my life at that early age. I wanted to scream at her, shake her, and tell her that she did not need my father. Long before I knew what feminism was, I knew one thing: I would never allow anyone to make me feel that way.

Eventually my father left, never to return. His addiction was out of control and his behavior was completely unpredictable. Sometimes I would go to wherever he was living to find him and the variety of people with him drugged out or sleeping all over the floor. Sometimes when he was sober, we would have fun adventures together—going to the Village, scouring the used-jewelry stores searching for silver and turquoise items or thumbing through the bins of vinyl records in the local record stores. My father loved music and had the uncanny ability to hear a song from a new artist and predict with incredible accuracy their eventual success. He was still prone to grand gestures, only this time they weren't romantic so much as hilarious and outrageous. Like when he turned up one day with a monkey he named Beau and explained that Beau was going to be living with him in his studio apartment, or the time he decorated his place with nothing but an aquarium full of piranhas. What could delight a rebellious teenager more than a father who loved rock and roll, made up his own rules, and took great pleasure in all things outrageous?

I wasn't naive or blind about who my father was. I reveled in the good times and endured the bad times. He was a mess, and I knew it. He was dangerous, and I felt it. But he was my father. And children love what they get. So when the late-night call came informing us that he had been arrested, it didn't change my feelings for him, only my level of concern. A little over a decade later, when I was beginning my career as a public defender, I would receive another late-night call from my cousin informing me that they had found his body, lifeless from a drug overdose that was likely intentional. Being his closest relative, I had to go down to the medical examiner's office to identify him. I hadn't seen him in a while, and I was surprised at how good he looked. His hair was a beautiful salt-and-pepper color, and he looked peaceful. Later on, I learned that they had found him with his headphones still on. He had been listening to *To Our Children's Children's Children*. The Moody Blues.

Watching my mother seemingly trapped by kids she didn't

really want and tethered to a marriage that not only crushed her potential as the "girl most likely to succeed" but also nearly broke her desire to live instilled in me the drive, independence, and tenacity to get what I wanted—even in the face of huge obstacles—traits that are essential when you are a woman in a male-dominated profession, and also when you are tasked with defending people at the mercy of the criminal justice system.

But it was my father who inadvertently taught me the most about what it means to be a public defender. Not because he cycled through the system or because he struggled with addiction and mental illness. What I learned from growing up with him is that you can love someone who lets you down. You can be loyal to someone who has done something terrible. And you can advocate for their dignity and worth, right up until the end, because they never cease to be a human being. I carried that lesson into every relationship with every client for over thirty-five years. Not because they reminded me of my father but because, like my father, they were entitled to be heard and seen in all their complexity and full humanity, not reduced to their worst moment or act.

I know what some of you may be thinking: that my decision to become a public defender was all about my father and that I am still subconsciously fighting for the man I couldn't save. It's an easy conclusion to draw, but it's wrong. In fact, I hid my father's story for most of my career, concerned that my resolve to challenge injustice would be misunderstood as a personal psychodrama rather than the political and moral imperative that it is. Every one of us should care about injustice and do something about it. Personal or lived experience certainly adds important perspective, but so long as you are willing to roll up your sleeves and do the work, there are no prerequisites to getting into this fight—at least not in my book.

What is true is that allowing yourself to love an unlovable person can teach you the courage to be vulnerable and not closed off to the suffering of another person, and this is the key to compassion.

But there's something else I learned from my childhood.

My two sets of grandparents could have easily hated each other. One set came from blue-collar coal-mining Pennsylvania. The other were upper-middle-class Jews. They voted differently. They dressed differently. My New York City grandparents traveled the world; my Pennsylvania grandparents barely left the front porch of their row house. They had entirely different worldviews. Under different circumstances, they never would have been able to see themselves in each other, but as life would have it, they got to see themselves *and each other* in me and my brother. This united them in purpose. They were on a mission to protect us and nurture us—the children of a doomed marriage—and they were not going to fail. For us, they learned to understand and respect each other. But because of us, they also came to love each other. Indeed, they stayed connected until the day they died.

It's a fascinating riddle how we turn out the way we do. Surely family and early personal experiences shape us more than we care to admit, as do the larger forces and contingencies of culture and society. Yet despite our differences, we share a common ground or human condition—one that is most clearly reflected when we see our children in others' children, and when we take responsibility for the world we are creating for them.

3

Fighting For versus Fighting Alongside

What type of person do you think of when you hear the words *convicted rapist*?

On the morning of November 10, 2014, Otis Prescot woke up in a dumpster.

Thousands of miles away, the Bronx was already alive and bustling. Our office, the Bronx Defenders, was a cacophony of lawyers and clients getting ready for court. I was sitting at my desk, sorting through paperwork and emails, when the phone rang.

"Hello, this is Robin."

The voice on the other end was unfamiliar, with a deep southern drawl. "Hi, ma'am. I'm calling because I've got someone here who says you know him, that you represented him. The gentleman's name is Otis Prescot."

I hadn't heard from Otis in a while. "I do know him. Is he okay?"

"Well, he's here with me. I found him sleeping in the dumpster next to the firehouse where I work. He told me that I could call you. I just want to give him something to eat, buy him a bus ticket, and send him on his way, but before I do, I want to make sure he's telling me the truth about who he is."

I quickly vouched for Otis and thanked the man—a firefighter, as he explained—for offering his help. The kindness of strangers.

"Okay, then, I don't know what he did to have you represent him, but no one should have to sleep in a dumpster."

I dwelled on his words for a moment after hanging up. We humans can be the kindest and the cruelest of creatures.

I had met Otis some twenty years earlier while working the night shift as a public defender in the Bronx criminal court. It was the 1990s and arrest rates were at an all-time high. Over the course of the night, court clerks would drop stack after stack of manila folders into the wire bins that sat on our desks. For each person who had been arrested within the past twenty-four hours, there was a packet stapled together that contained a rap sheet, a recommendation for release/nonrelease, and the criminal complaint—the document that laid out the charges against the accused and the facts that supported them.

We were supposed to select packets from the bin at random.

After all, it was our duty to defend anyone, for anything, anytime. That is the essence of being a public defender. But the truth is, we cherry-picked . . . to some extent. This wasn't about our own personal feelings or inklings about the charges or the person involved. It was because for even the most passionate public defender, the crush of police arrests for minor offenses that never should have been brought into the system in the first place created a kind of disheartening monotony. At the time, "broken windows" policing—the theory that by targeting small offenses, such as weed smoking or turnstile jumping, you could prevent serious crime—was growing in popularity, and people in New York City, particularly in communities of color, were being arrested left and right for ever more minor offenses. As a result, out of dozens of cases, perhaps only a few required nuanced lawyering. So we looked for the more challenging cases in addition to our regular share, hoping to put our actual training to use.

I can't remember if I intentionally selected Otis's case or not, but I will never forget our first meeting.

I stood in front of the "pens," the unofficial name court staff use for the small, windowless jail cells in the courthouse. In the pens, people await their first court appearance, when the charges against them are read aloud and bail is set.

Many nights, the cells were so crowded that men slept under the benches or on the sticky cement floor. The fluorescent lights flickered all night long and the air smelled like a combination of oranges and urine. Everything echoed—voices, the TV that blared all night and was strategically placed so only corrections officers could watch it, and the sound of huge metal doors slamming open and shut as people were led in and out of the cells.

"Otis Prescot," I called out. The men in the cell looked up and shifted in their seats. A tall, thin Black man with a 1970s look nodded in acknowledgment and walked up to me.

"I'm Otis Prescot," he said.

"Hi, Mr. Prescot. I'm Robin Steinberg and I'm going to be your lawyer on this case. Let's talk in a more private place."

The corrections officer led us to a small metal table reserved for lawyers to meet with their clients before appearing in front of the judge.

"Mr. Prescot, do you know what the police charged you with?"

"Yes, but I didn't do it." He looked directly into my eyes. There was an uncomfortable pause, one that I knew all too well from my years representing men charged with sexual assault.

Sensing his concern, I put the paperwork aside for a moment. "Mr. Prescot, I don't know how you feel about having a woman attorney represent you in this case. If I were you, I might worry that because you are charged with rape, I might not fight as hard for you as a man attorney, especially because I see from your rap sheet that you have a prior conviction for rape and are still on parole for that. But nothing could be further from the truth. I don't care what you have been charged with or what you might have done in your past. I'm just here to defend you and fight for you on this case, and I promise you that's what I'll do."

He studied me carefully. "Why do you do this work, Miss

Steinberg?" No client had ever asked me that question before. I hesitated, recognizing the importance of my answer.

"I hate unfairness, Mr. Prescot. And everything about how this system operates is unfair. It's that simple."

Truth is, it wasn't simple at all. Nothing about how we end up doing the things we do ever is.

I explained to Otis that during this first court appearance, the prosecutor would read the charges, and the judge would set bail. I prepared him for what he already knew. The judge would set bail very high, given the nature of the case, and it was likely that the parole department would drop a "hold" on him, making it impossible for him to get out while the current case was pending, even if he could get help posting the bail. If he wanted to take the case to trial, which he did, he would be held in jail at Rikers Island for as long as it took to secure a trial date, which could be a year or more.

"Mr. Prescot, one of the things that we have to decide right away is whether or not you want to testify in front of the grand jury."

In New York, when someone is arrested and charged with a felony, a grand jury must hear evidence to determine if there is cause to believe the accused has committed the crime. If there is, the grand jury will return an indictment and the criminal process will continue. It is a closed-door proceeding that any reasonable observer would recognize is one-sided.

The prosecutor presents their evidence, there is no defense lawyer to cross-examine witnesses, and the accused can't hear what the witnesses say against them. The accused has a right to testify, under oath, in front of the grand jury, but the process is completely controlled by the prosecutor. Defense counsel is obligated to tell their client that they have the "right" to testify in front of the grand jury. And so, as I had done thousands of times before, I advised Mr. Prescot that he had the right to testify.

Truth is, I didn't want him to testify. At this point, all he could say was "I didn't do it"—hardly persuasive enough to convince a grand jury to let him go home. I couldn't see the upside, even though not testifying guaranteed an indictment would be filed against him and he would have to wait for his trial. The downside of testifying was that he would open himself up to a wide-ranging cross-examination by the prosecutor, and anything he said could be used against him later. Unlike the accused, the person who brings the accusation isn't cross-examined by anyone, since defense counsel is not allowed to actively participate in the proceeding. As Sol Wachtler, a former chief judge of New York State, once said, prosecutors have so much influence on grand juries that they could get them to "indict a ham sandwich."[1] From a legal point of view, it was a terrible idea, and I told him so.

"I want to testify," he insisted. Recognizing that I didn't have enough time to persuade him, I promised to schedule a meeting with him soon so we could discuss it further. Establishing trust with your client is critical when you are a public defender. But it takes time and patience—hardly the hallmarks of most public defenders, who work frantically under heavy caseloads.

At our next meeting, we got to know each other better and discussed again whether he should testify. I continued to impress upon him how one-sided the grand jury process was and that it was a terrible idea to go in front of them. He would not be deterred.

I could not understand why a man as smart as Otis clearly was would want to commit what—from my perspective—was legal suicide. "It makes no sense, Mr. Prescot," I pleaded, and repeated all the reasons why. But he held fast. At last, growing increasingly frustrated, I called an end to our meeting and stormed out. Not my best moment.

I went home that night and mulled over the conversation. How could I persuade him? Whom could I enlist to support my argument? He had no family that I could call, no friends to approach, and his girlfriend was the mother of the young girl who had accused him of rape, so contacting her would not help. I could call in a colleague to reiterate what I was saying so he could see that this was standard legal advice for this type of case, but I had an intuition that perhaps I had more in common with Otis than most of my younger colleagues did. Perhaps I could find a way to have more influence, if only I found the right approach.

Like me, Otis was a child of the sixties. Despite our differences— race, gender, experience in the criminal justice system—we had some shared cultural references. We loved Jimi Hendrix. We played the guitar. We liked seventies fashion. It was the nineties, and we were already reminiscing about New York City "back in the day," comparing our favorite places and sharing stories. He was fond of telling me that he was happy that I was Jewish because he had once had a beloved boss who was also Jewish. And so he called me "Boss" too. As I went to sleep that night, I could not stop thinking about why he wouldn't take my advice.

I sleep easily at night, usually. But when I awake, I often have fully formed ideas and thoughts in my head. I tell people that there must be little women who stay up all night long working, thinking, and problem-solving inside my head as I sleep. Those women were definitely at work that night, mulling over why my meeting with Otis had become so contentious and what had gone wrong. When I woke up, the answer was clear as day—a revelation so obvious that I was shocked by my own arrogance and ignorance.

For all that Otis and I had in common, the thing we did not share, the reality I could not even imagine, was the experience of being *silenced* just by virtue of being a Black man in America. Otis just wanted to be heard. It was that simple. He could not tolerate being silenced one more time. He needed to tell his story, on his own terms, and he was willing to suffer whatever legal consequences might come. And while I knew that the legal risk to him was high, I felt that I understood, perhaps for the first time, the significance of his decision. For Otis, speaking, telling his story, being heard, was an act of resistance to a system that, in every interaction throughout his life, seemed designed to silence him, cage him, and destroy him. The cost of staying silent was higher than I had ever understood. I was embarrassed that this revelation had taken me so long and grateful to Otis for awakening me.

At our next meeting, I apologized for not hearing him, for not respecting his decision or understanding why speaking out was so important to him. Otis smiled knowingly. From that moment on, I vowed to fight *alongside* Otis, not *for* him. And that is a lesson I have taken into my work as an advocate ever since. Two days later, we marched into the grand jury together.

The law in New York says that defense counsel may not speak in the grand jury but can be present while the accused testifies. Otis and I agreed on a silent code to communicate during the proceedings. If things were going badly, I would drop my pen and that would be a signal for Otis to request a break to speak with me outside. I never had to drop my pen—his testimony was compelling and focused.

Otis explained that his girlfriend's daughter had fabricated this accusation because she wanted them to separate and because she had recently learned about his past and knew that made him vulnerable. Decades earlier, Otis had been convicted of rape, a charge he denied from the first day I met him until his very last day. He did his time in prison, got out, and went on with his life. He fell in love with his girlfriend and moved into her home in the Bronx. But her daughter didn't like Otis. He was strict and wanted her to be accountable for her rash teenage behavior. She wanted him gone, and so she told her mother that Otis had raped her.

Not surprisingly, the grand jury indicted Otis. But what was a surprise was how long the decision to indict him took. Clearly, there must have been a debate about whose story to believe. This gave us hope that when we finally got to trial, and I had an opportunity to cross-examine the accuser, we could win.

More important, Otis and I were now partners in his defense. Over the many months of preparation for trial, Otis and I got to know each other better. We shared personal stories, read *Zen and the Art of Motorcycle Maintenance* together, and enjoyed our frequent trips down rock-and-roll memory lane.

His trust in me grew, and my admiration of his intelligence, fearlessness, and resilience flourished. It took us almost a year to get his trial date. Court delays in the Bronx were notorious back then and have remained an issue. In fact, in 2016, the Bronx Defenders had to sue the governor of New York and the administrators of the court system for failing to ensure speedy trials and due process for people in the Bronx, a constitutional requirement. Many of our clients in the Bronx waited months if not years to go to trial, and for those who could not afford bail and were stuck at Rikers Island or the Vernon Correctional Center, also known as "the Boat" (it is literally a floating jail), the pressure to take a guilty plea was tremendous.

Otis had to remain in jail the entire time, unable to make the $50,000 cash bail the judge had set. This was more money than he made in an entire year, and he had no one who could help. Otis turned down every plea offer for a lesser sentence made by the prosecutor, even knowing that if convicted, he faced up to twenty-five years in prison, in addition to even more jail time for violating his parole on the previous conviction by having a new arrest. The rest of his life was at risk.

On the first day of the trial, Otis was buoyant and confident. "Ready, Boss?" he asked me as the court officers brought him in in handcuffs. "Absolutely, Otis," I replied, masking my internal terror.

There has never been a time when I was not filled with anxiety and fear as I was about to start a trial with a client. By the time trials roll around, good public defenders have gotten to know their clients, and the clients' families, well. The pressure to win—and get your client free—isn't political or theoretical; it is personal. Of course, clients and their loved ones bear the devastating burden of a loss, but public defenders carry the responsibility. I adored Otis, and the thought that he might spend the rest of his life in prison if I couldn't convince the jury of his innocence haunted me.

The trial lasted only a week. Our jury was a diverse group of people from the Bronx who listened—at every stage—with exactly the kind of attention that a life-altering decision warrants. But no matter how hard I tried, I couldn't read their expressions or get any signal about what they were thinking. When the teenage daughter of Otis's girlfriend got up on the stand, all eyes were on her. At the prosecutor's prompting, she told the story of her alleged rape clearly and without emotion.

According to the teen, she was taking a nap in the living room in middle of the day, as her mom napped in the bedroom nearby. She was wearing a T-shirt and denim short shorts. She said when she woke up, her shorts and underwear were pulled to her ankles and Otis was climbing off her.

Next it was time for me to cross-examine her. I started by asking her about her relationship with Otis and how much she didn't like his strict rules. That established a potential motive to make up the story. I knew where I had to go from there.

On the day you say this happened, you were sixteen years old, correct?

You were about five foot four inches tall then?

And you weighed about a hundred and sixty pounds?

When you fell asleep on the couch in the living room, you were wearing blue-jean short shorts, right?

And they had a zipper up the front?

And when you fell asleep, your shorts were zipped closed?

And you also had on underwear?

Now, let me understand. When Otis unzipped your shorts, you didn't wake up?

When Otis pulled down your shorts, you didn't wake up?

When he removed your underwear, you didn't wake up?

When he got on top of you, you didn't wake up?

When he put his penis inside your vagina, you didn't wake up?

When he was raping you, you didn't wake up?

Your story is that it was only after he finished raping you, and was climbing off of you, that you finally woke up?

And that was when you realized that you had been raped?

She responded to each of my questions with a simple "Yes" or "That's right." I couldn't help but feel sad for her. I'm sure she thought that once she made the allegation, her mother would throw Otis out of the house and that would be the end of it. She probably never imagined that they would end up in a court, much less a trial.

Truth is, less than 5 percent of cases in the Bronx ever went to trial.[2] This largely mirrored a national trend that continues to this day. As the title of a 2016 *New York Times* piece on this issue put it, "trial by jury, a hallowed American right, is vanishing."[3] The criminal justice system is supposed to be a place to adjudicate facts, law, and justice, but it has long since become a plea factory, a system where the court process itself, before conviction, often feels like the punishment. From the moment a judge sets cash bail without regard for what you can pay to the plea "deals" offered along the way, all the incentives are to plead guilty.

While the right to a trial is fundamental to justice, the system punishes those who insist on it by sentencing them more harshly after trial than if they had pleaded guilty. I have stood next to countless clients as judges warned them about the cost of going to trial. "Sir, I must tell you that if you insist on going to trial, my offer of sentencing you to one year in jail goes away, and if you are convicted, you face up to fifteen years in prison. Of course, the choice is entirely yours." This plea discount—or "trial tax," as many public defenders call it—is meant to discourage people from seeking trials, because if everyone did, the court system would quickly become overwhelmed and come to a crashing halt.

But that pressure would not work on Otis, not even when, on the eve of trial, the prosecutor offered him a two-year sentence, which at that point, with "good time" credit, would have meant he had to serve only an additional six months. Despite the nights in jail and the prospect of getting up to twenty-five years, he held on to his innocence.

The trial was finally coming to an end, and we had one final major decision to make: Should Otis take the stand? I felt confident that we had laid bare the gaps and impossibility of the accuser's story, but since you never know for sure what a jury is thinking, we had to decide *together* whether or not he should testify.

Anyone accused of a crime has the constitutional right to remain silent. At the beginning and end of a trial, judges instruct jurors that no negative inference can be drawn from that silence. But jurors always want to hear both sides of the story; it's human nature. I turned to Otis and, having learned my lesson earlier, asked, "What are you thinking about whether or not you want to testify?" He replied quickly, looking me square in the face, "I don't know, Boss. What do you think?" I smiled, realizing how far we had come together and how much trust and mutual respect we now had for each other.

"I know it's a hard thing to not tell your story, Otis, but I think we have done all we can to show how incredible her story is. I don't see a lot of upside to subjecting yourself to questioning, especially because the judge ruled that they can cross-examine you about having a prior conviction. Right now, the jury has no idea." It was too risky, and I knew it, but I was ready to support whatever decision he made. "Okay, you're the boss," he said. And with that, the evidentiary part of the trial was over.

The last thing a defense lawyer gets to do in a criminal trial is give a summation. It's where we get to bring all the facts together and try to persuade the jury to acquit our clients. It is my absolute favorite part of a trial. Not just because it signals that the trial is coming to an end and I might finally be able to sleep at night again, or because it is the one time that I can actually control—completely—what is happening in the courtroom, but because it is the moment when I can use all of my passion and skills as an attorney and storyteller to persuade a jury to do the right thing. And it's the opportunity to really show my client how much I believe in them, and to stand up not just for the legal case but for that person's humanity.

I approached the jury and began with a fairy tale: "Once upon a time, in a faraway land . . ." I'm quite certain that Otis thought I had lost my mind, but then he saw where I was going. The jury did too. The story, as told by this troubled teenager, was as incredible as a fairy tale—only tragic.

They watched as I recounted the alleged events and pointed out the absurdities and impossibilities. They tracked me as I walked across the courtroom, and they didn't blink when I walked over to Otis and put my hands on his shoulders and asked them to see this prosecution for what it was—a complete fabrication and an affront to their intelligence. Find Mr. Prescot not guilty, I ended.

And they did.

At 3:45 p.m. on the Friday before the Fourth of July, Otis Prescot walked free for the first time in a year. For once, I felt somewhat optimistic about the practice of law in an adversarial system. As we walked down the steps of the courthouse onto 161st Street in the Bronx, I couldn't help but marvel at the idea of putting such a life-altering decision in the hands of twelve strangers. Despite all the failures, all the injustice, and all the racism I had seen in the system, for this moment, as we breathed fresh air together, I was a believer that there was still room for justice.

Otis and I went back to my office, which was right down the street from the courthouse. He had nothing but the clothes he had been wearing when they arrested him. At the Bronx Defenders we had established years earlier a client clothes closet for just these moments. Otis and I searched through the closet and found some jeans, a summer-weight shirt, and a pair of sneakers that he could wear as he stared down this first night of freedom. I was almost giddy with delight and relief. When it was time to say goodbye, Otis assured me that he had a friend he could stay with for the night. I wasn't at all sure, and I suspected that he would find his way to one of the many shelters in New York City for the weekend, ashamed to tell me that he had no one and nowhere to go.

"You sure you don't need anything else?" I asked stupidly. I knew what he needed. He needed the clock turned back. He needed that first conviction—from all those years ago, for a rape that he swore he didn't do, that sent him to prison for more than a decade—erased. He needed the years he had aged in prison to be wound back. He needed the criminal record that followed him, limiting his employment opportunities, erased. And now, having spent a year in jail and lost everything again, he needed a job, a home, a family, and a future.

In that moment, those truths went unspoken. Instead, I reminded him that he had to report to his parole officer first thing after the holiday weekend when the courts and administrative offices reopened. If he didn't do that, I told him, his parole would be violated, and they would send him back to jail. Then I wished him a happy Fourth of July, gave him my personal phone number in case he wanted to speak to me over the weekend, and told him what an honor it was to represent him. "Thanks, Boss. I'll come see you after I see my PO on Tuesday." And with that, we parted ways.

Otis and I had managed to face down the system this time. But it was short-lived. When I returned to work on Tuesday morning, I got the call: "Boss, I'm at the parole office. They're arresting me." I grabbed my things in a rush and headed to the parole office. When I arrived, Otis was in handcuffs, chained to a metal chair next to the parole officer's desk.

"I'm Mr. Prescot's lawyer. Why are you arresting him?"

His parole officer, a middle-aged, dispassionate woman who had all the signs of having been in the system too long, barely looked up at me. "He failed to report to the parole office on time."

I stared at her in disbelief, my blood pressure rising. "What? He got here first thing this morning. He was released from jail after being found *not guilty* late on Friday afternoon, he came to my office to get some clothes, but it was already the end of the day. What did you expect him to do?" My voice was getting loud, and I knew that I had to get control of myself.

"Well," she said, "he should have come over here right after he was released. He had time. We are open until five p.m." I stood there, speechless. "Given the nature of his offense, Counselor, you should have advised him better."

I felt the shame of being part of this horrendous system, even if my role was to defend those most vulnerable against it. I wondered if this was my fault. Would she have violated his parole if, rather than come to my office for fresh clothes and a MetroCard to travel with, he had shown up at her office at 5:00 p.m. on the Friday before the Fourth of July? I knew in my heart that there was zero chance she had been anywhere near her office then, but I felt responsible for giving her the ammunition. Otis was eerily calm, and his resignation startled me. After all, he was the guy who had risked it all, who had insisted on telling his story to the grand jury, who had faced down the false accusations and put his fate in the hands of twelve strangers. But he was also a Black man in a system designed to capture him, and he knew it. As they walked him by me in handcuffs, on his way to jail again, he looked directly at me. "At least I had the weekend," he said with a faint smile. And with that, he was gone.

The system ended up taking another year from Otis's life. It didn't happen because they found him guilty of failing to report to the parole office that Friday afternoon after his acquittal. It happened because during the parole hearing, which I was confident we would win, Otis finally cracked. He just couldn't take it anymore. He called the judge overseeing the hearing a choice expletive, and she, in turn, held him in contempt and sentenced him to a year.

He did his time, writing me letters from jail regularly. He did not have a shred of regret about what happened. Like that time when he insisted on telling his story to the grand jury, he just needed to fight back and speak out, and he was willing to pay the price. Over and over again. It was just one of the many things that made me love him so.

When Otis finished his yearlong sentence, he lived in the Bronx for a while. He came by my office every now and then—sometimes just to check in, sometimes to talk about deeper issues, and sometimes, when I wasn't there, he would leave me a small gift. Usually a bottle of Charlie perfume. The younger public defenders in my office had never heard of Charlie, since it was a perfume sold widely in the seventies, an era that Otis and I shared and often discussed. I'm sure that some of my colleagues thought it was creepy that a "sex offender" would leave the executive director of their office perfume, but I understood that it was Otis's way of sharing with me a certain nostalgia for that era, before the system came crashing down on him, when life seemed to be just about music, dance, and the hope for revolutionary change. That perfume, left on my chair, was his way of reminding me that once, a long time ago, he was not the person that the system now defined him to be. I lined those perfume bottles up on the windowsill in my office. They reminded me that despite the horrors the system inflicts on people, humanity can never be taken away.

Over the years that followed, Otis traveled around the country. He was violating his parole, and he knew it, but playing by their rules was now impossible for him. He would call me from time to time. Mostly just to say hi but sometimes to tell me where he was and share a new adventure with me. I knew that he was struggling and I worried about him. So when the firefighter called me after finding him asleep in the dumpster, I was relieved to know that he was alive.

The next time I heard from him was when he called to ask if he would bring more attention to himself if he walked into Mexico or rode his bicycle across the border. He knew that if government officials ran his name, they might find out that he was wanted in New York for failing to report to parole as a "registered sex offender" from the conviction decades ago. I advised him to walk. "Okay, Boss, walk it is."

That was the last I heard from Otis. I hoped that somehow he had made it into Mexico, had replaced the bicycle he left on the other side of the border, had fallen in love, had found a job, and was living happily in a place where no one defined him by his past and people accepted him for the brilliant, quirky, guitar-playing, resilient soul I knew him to be.

I could have allowed the label "rapist" to prevent me from getting to know the Otis I knew. I could have done my job, tried his case, and fulfilled my obligations as his court-appointed counselor, but I would have missed the richness of who he was and the importance of entering into that space of shared humanity where the voice of another can actually be heard. Once you do that, you move from feeling mere sympathy to experiencing compassion—and there is no turning back.

From time to time, I would run his name in the computer to see if he had been rearrested. Nothing. Until one day, I ran across a newspaper article with the headline MAN ON BICYCLE KILLED ON I-25 NEAR SAN ANTONIO. The story explained that the bicyclist was accidentally struck by a twenty-five-year-old young man and that "the victim was identified as Otis Prescot, who just celebrated his 56th birthday."

I sat silently until I began to cry—for the tragedy of his death, of course, and for the senselessness of his end, but more than anything because finally, and ironically, in death Otis got what he had fought for his entire life—one moment of being seen as just that: a man, not a label or criminal record.

4

Throwing Stones versus Befriending the King[1]

Long before Otis, and long before criminal court became my battleground, my idea of how I wanted to change the world was quite different. Judging by the 1960s icons (like Gloria Steinem, Angela Davis, and Malcolm X) whom, as a teenager, I glued onto the pages of my treasured blue denim scrapbook, the last thing I would have imagined was that all my rebellious energy would eventually lead me to be a lawyer. But that's what it did. The question I asked myself then, as I still do now, is simple: Where can I make a difference? It's a question each of us must answer individually when considering what role to play in the struggles for equality, human dignity, and justice.

There's no wrong answer; there just needs to be one, for we all must do our part.

My political journey began in college. To say that I wasn't college-bound would be an understatement. Neither of my parents graduated from college, and given our home life, higher education was not exactly a hot topic of conversation. But as fate would have it, while my father was out on his journey of self-destruction, my mother fell for a man in California who promised her love, security, and a future.

One day toward the end of junior year of high school, my mother announced that we were moving to California to join her future husband. Moving a teenager in her last year of high school away from her friends, beloved grandparents, and life in the only city she has ever known as home was a questionable parenting decision, even if that's what my mother needed to do for her own well-being. One thing it accomplished for sure was catalyzing my rebellious streak. And rebellious I was.

Landing in Los Angeles in the fall of 1974 with my ten-year-old brother, Robert, in tow, we were picked up by my mother's boyfriend and taken to our new home. It was a small, one-level house on a street called Bundy Drive with a lemon tree in the tiny front yard. My brother didn't know what was happening to him, since my mother had decided to keep it all a secret, telling him instead that we were going on vacation. I knew it was more than that, but she insisted I keep her secret so she could start a new life, away from the insecurity and misery of her existence in New

York City. The truth was that she wanted to ensure that my father couldn't find us. Not knowing our address, he sent letters to us through her lawyer, but she did not mention it, allowing us to believe that he didn't care about us in the slightest. My brother and I never quite forgave her for that.

I was determined to be miserable. That would be my revenge. Classic teenager. I wore New York City clothes—long-sleeved sweaters, jeans, and work boots—in the California heat. I gave up food for coffee and took up cigarettes. I listened to protest music and swore off most adults. They weren't to be trusted. By the time I started my senior year at my new high school, I was a teacher's nightmare.

But life has always had a way of leading me to the right person at the right time.

Against my will, the school made me take an English class in order to graduate. The only other mandate was that I take a "life skills" class (I took typing) and driver's education (a bewildering idea to a kid from New York City). I will never know what prompted her to pay attention to me, but in that first week of school, the English teacher, who I would later learn went by "Mama Rose," asked me to stay after class. When the other students left, she stood up and walked over to where I was seated. Looking me square in the eyes, she said, "I can see that you aren't like most of these kids. How did you wind up here, and what's going on with you?"

My usual instinct to keep quiet and avoid personal disclosure suddenly gave way, and I found myself pouring my heart, and my unhappiness, out to this tiny old woman with a deep, raspy voice, thick glasses, and a biting wit. I don't remember if I cried as I told her my story, but when I finally stopped talking, she sat for a moment, silently studying me and nodding ever so slightly. Then she got up from her chair, walked over to her desk, and picked up a book. "Here. Let's start with this. Read it. I think you'll like it, and it's better than the stuff I assign in this class. Stick close to me and we will get you through this year."

I looked down at the cover of the book and read the title, *A Doll's House*. I had no idea what the book was about, or that it would be my first introduction to feminism as an intellectual journey rather than an emotional response to the world around me. With that small gesture of kindness and belief in me, Mama Rose changed the course of my life.

That year, I lost myself in books. After school, I went directly to my part-time job at a local grocery store, where I took pleasure in bagging groceries and in my end-of-shift ritual of spraying the massive produce section with cool water to ensure that it stayed fresh for the next day's customers. I had never seen half the things that were lined up on those shelves—who knew there was more to nature than iceberg lettuce and canned pineapple? Arranging the produce and nurturing it with cold-water mist at night gave me a surprising sense of satisfaction. It gave me a sense of control and predictability when everything else was shifting under my feet and I had no idea where I would ultimately land.

At night, I would read the books that Mama Rose gave me. I would lie awake, thinking about each new idea and underlining the passages that meant the most to me, so that we could discuss them at our meetings.

Mama Rose asked me to put my thoughts on paper, and so, for the first time, someone encouraged me to use writing as an outlet to express my ideas. Draft after draft, Mama Rose would take her red Magic Marker and show me how to improve. After our sessions, she would say, "Bubbala, when you get to college next year, you are going to need to know how to write."

Truth was, I hadn't given much thought to college. It was hard to see myself as part of an elite group of young people, and I desperately wanted to go "home" to New York City. I think she knew both those things. So rather than delve into why I hadn't charted a path to college or psychoanalyze my perpetual self-doubt and homesickness, she simply articulated her clear *expectation* that I would be going to college. Whether it was the power of her suggestion or my desire to please her I will never know, but suddenly I began to imagine myself on a college campus.

Months later when my mother's boyfriend, who later that year became my stepfather, asked where I wanted to go to college, I knew exactly where I wanted to be: Berkeley. Truthfully, I had no idea that Berkeley was an extraordinary academic institution. I didn't even know that it was part of the vast, incredible University of California system of higher education. I just knew that it was one of the epicenters of student activism and radical thinking at the time, and I wanted to be part of it.

Arriving at Berkeley in the fall of 1975, I soon learned about a program called Strawberry Creek College, an alternative school within Berkeley, if there could be such a thing. Thumbing through the catalog of classes, I was intrigued by the course offerings—things like "Women in China," "Radical Education," and "The Rise of the Multinational Corporation." I was hooked.

Strawberry Creek College was contained in an old, gray, wooden two-story structure in the middle of campus by a small stream called, well, Strawberry Creek. The building had been an ROTC structure before student activists opposing the Vietnam War pushed them off campus. I was delighted by the symbolism of taking over an ROTC building to educate young people on how to question power.

I started classes in January at Strawberry Creek and blossomed, despite a rocky start where I adamantly refused to participate in a "trust game" where students and faculty stood in a circle and one by one took turns going into the middle, closing their eyes, and falling backward—"trusting" that a random classmate or faculty member would catch them. Were these people insane?

By today's standards, almost everything about Strawberry Creek would be unacceptable, outrageous, and lawsuit-worthy. There were student-faculty romances, skinny-dipping at the head of school's home, and countless potluck suppers where we all drank too much wine and smoked too much weed. Looking back, it may have been completely inappropriate. But for me, it was the intellectual and emotional journey of a lifetime. I thrived in the small seminars. There were new ideas, interesting conversations, and heated debates about political revolution. We went to concerts in small venues around the East Bay, listening to local musicians who channeled social critique into lyrics, and watched countless documentary films. I developed a deeper, conscious political framework that explained the world I knew and helped inspire in me the desire to create a better one.

I know that it might sound like I was turning into the classic lefty, tie-dye-loving Berkeley hippie—and I sure dressed the part—but no sooner had I found my social clique than a growing skepticism began to grow in me. Certainly I reveled in the intellectual conversations about social struggle and political change, and the sense of comradery, but my distrust of authority ran deep, and I recoiled at the slightest whiff of groupthink and intellectual orthodoxy. The academic approach seemed at times too abstract, too one-dimensional, even a little dogmatic and more concerned with political purity than with efficacy. I craved something more pragmatic. What was the use of all this talk if the only strategy to challenge power was throwing stones from the outside? There had to be more to it, so I rushed to find the answer.

Anyone who has ever worked with me knows that I work at a frantic pace. That started at Berkeley when I began to have academic success. The better I got at something and the more I accomplished, the more I pushed myself. It was almost as if I feared that it would all disappear if I ever stopped to catch my breath. That feeling has never left me. To this day, I never trust my successes. I never reflect on them for more than a moment and never allow them to become part of my consciousness and certainly not part of my identity. Perhaps it's perpetual self-doubt from a childhood filled with insecurity and abandonment. Perhaps it's a sense that I never really belong anywhere, given my family background and suddenly being ripped out of New York (we're all products of our upbringing, aren't we?). Maybe it's impostor syndrome, never really accepting that I am smart or capable enough. Or maybe it's because I have learned that women must work harder, faster, and with more competence than men if they want to be taken seriously. Whatever drove me then, and still compels me now, led me to finish my degree in women's studies in just over three years and quickly face the question: Now what?

I sat with the question for some time. Should I join the ranks of activists to raise awareness and push for social justice? Should I continue academic studies and train other young people to develop the intellectual tools to question ingrained ideologies and power structures? Everyone around me seemed to be flocking into one of these two camps.

I knew I wanted to fight for women's rights. And I knew I wanted a seat at the table. But most important, my intuition told me that if I truly wanted to transform the systems that perpetuated inequality and injustice, I had to begin by understanding them from the inside out. There's more than one way to have a revolution—and context matters. Sometimes standing outside the palace walls and throwing stones at windows is effective. Other times, it may be better to find your way into the palace, "befriend the king," and learn the ropes. And sometimes it's better to be a Trojan horse. For the kind of systemic change I wanted to effect, I needed to be on the inside. So I decided to go to law school.

It wasn't an obvious choice, and people who knew me were shocked by my decision. Some even labeled me a sellout and questioned my commitment to change. It was a fair question. Certainly, law school is about the most conservative, mainstream endeavor one can engage in. And once you make the decision to go, you have crossed a bridge. You are joining a field that is built largely on maintaining the status quo and a profession that protects the interests of the most powerful among us, often at the expense of the least powerful.

But what is also true is that in order to create social change, you need more than catchy slogans. You have to understand power. Our system of laws was designed to create and maintain a certain power structure. In my young mind, law school was a way to learn how to navigate that structure and understand its levers and fault lines. It was a way to acquire new tools. Nothing more and nothing less.

In the fall of 1979, I traded my tie-dyes and peasant skirts for pants and blazers and began classes at NYU School of Law. I was accustomed to feeling like a fish out of water for much of my life, so there was nothing new about the range of emotions I felt during those early days at NYU.

Looking around at my classmates, I couldn't have felt more ill at ease. I don't know what it was exactly. After all, women made up almost half the class, students were overwhelmingly white, and all were overachievers. There was nothing on the surface that should have made me feel so different. Perhaps it was their affinity for white wine, their legacy parents, or their focus on grades, law review, federal clerkships, and big law firms. I needed my own crew.

I quickly identified students I could connect with—a brilliant, funny feminist who was a cartoonist and great baseball player; a skeptical, bridge-playing daughter of a doctor who challenged gender norms of any kind; a smart, kind, high-achieving woman from very modest roots in Virginia; and a brilliant intellectual from Brooklyn who had deep working-class roots that included a father who was an NYPD detective and a mother who worked as a bank teller, and who, like me, preferred Jack Daniel's to white wine. I could not have survived law school without these women, and more than forty years later, I still adore them.

In law school, I learned how to "think like a lawyer"—a unique perspective that taught you to analyze facts, apply guiding principles, and develop the tools to argue any side, without regard to political beliefs or even what was right. There was no right or wrong, only two sides to a given argument. I didn't believe that for a minute, but I quickly learned how to spit back the orthodoxy of law school with ease.

I was beginning to understand how important it was—when you go inside any system or institution—to know your values, to have principles, and to hold on to your ideals for the type of society you want to live in. It is possible to work for change within any power structure—even the most hateful ones—without becoming an accomplice. But it requires personal vigilance, courage, self-knowledge, and a clear sense of the lines you will—and won't—cross. Without that compass, you run the risk of being swallowed up by the very system you abhor.

My time with the Women's Prison Project, the law school clinic I mentioned earlier, helped me define those lines. Not only did the women at Bedford Hills Correctional Facility inspire my journey into public defense, but the experience fine-tuned my moral compass. It confirmed for me the strategic value of "hacking" into the system to fight alongside those most directly impacted by it, and it taught me to think concretely about the endgame. To this day, whenever I struggle with a decision at the organizational level, I always seek clarity in the answer to one question: Does it benefit our clients?

After the Women's Prison Project, I applied for an internship at the Southern Poverty Law Center in Montgomery, Alabama. I had never been to the American South, and I was thrilled to join a deeply respected civil rights organization filled with dedicated and talented lawyers fighting racial injustice under the most challenging circumstances.

On a hot summer day, I set out in my old blue Peugeot for Alabama. I barely stopped along the way, choosing to drive all day and night and braking only for gas and to use a bathroom at a truck stop. When I finally arrived, I was greeted by the lawyer who would supervise my work and who graciously put me up in his home until I could find a place of my own.

Steve was super smart, considerate, thoughtful, dedicated, and polite in a midwestern kind of way. He invited me to join the legal team working on a sentence-mitigation strategy on behalf of a young Black man in Starkville, Mississippi, who, during the course of a robbery, panicked and fatally shot the white woman who was the cashier.

A jury had already found him guilty. Now that the battle for his liberty was lost, the battle for his life began. There were only two possible outcomes: life in prison or death.

The day of sentencing, armed officers greeted us outside the courthouse and escorted us into the building. It was brutally hot, even at 8:00 a.m. Massive fans swung overhead, cutting through the hot air and the palpable tension in the room. We took our place at the defense table and watched as the small courtroom filled up with spectators.

On one side were Black community members, including our client's family. On the other, the family of the murdered woman and other white townspeople. The scene was right out of *To Kill a Mockingbird*, a movie I watched countless times as a teenager. Unlike Tom Robinson, our client was not wrongfully convicted of the crime. He did kill the woman, and the only thing left to decide was whether this young man would live.

I have always been confused by the idea of the death penalty. But up until then, that confusion had been largely intellectual— why give government the power to take away not just liberty but life? Why take such a risk? As I sat next to our young client, my stomach wrenched in knots of anger and despair as my understanding of what such power truly meant turned personal and visceral. Certainly he had committed a horrible crime that left a family grief-stricken and devastated, but I just couldn't understand how leaving his family equally broken and devastated would serve justice. He was at the beginning of his life. Were we really going to end it? Weren't we supposed to show mercy? Wasn't that the lesson of all those crucifixes adorning necks and walls?

It was clear this wasn't about justice. It was about retribution. In that moment I was thankful for those who dedicate their lives to learn law in order to stand alongside a person when the power of the state can take their life. Their preparation paid off. The sentencing advocacy was brilliant, and it worked. The jury spared the young man's life, a life that would still be spent entirely in a Mississippi prison.

It was a tremendous legal victory, considering that the only other option was the electric chair. But that night at the celebratory dinner we had in the home of the local lawyer, I couldn't stop the sadness that crept up on me between toasts. It was the first of many legal "victories" for clients that left me feeling unsatisfied.

Even though I was left with more questions than answers about our society's approach to punishment, I had no reservations about the lawyers I interned for at the organization. My usual skepticism of people in authority soon gave way to a growing admiration for them and their courageous work. They were quickly becoming my social justice heroes. But as with all self-created myths, the light of reality soon hit me. This time it was outside a courtroom, but it taught me everything I needed to know about power, leadership, and the realities of being a woman in a world of men.

The Southern Poverty Law Center was founded by a social justice icon, Morris Dees. A white southerner himself, he spent his life working to end racial injustice in the South. He was a hero to many and a target of intense hatred to others, who saw him as a "race traitor." He seemed to know everyone, including nationally recognized elected officials like Julian Bond and John Lewis, who stopped by to see him when visiting Montgomery. He was a legend. And so, when he asked me to join him on a visit to speak with a couple outside town about a lawsuit, I jumped at the chance to learn from him.

It didn't strike me as odd that the visit was scheduled for a Saturday. After all, the lawyers worked around the clock. But when he pulled up outside my rented apartment on his motorcycle, I was surprised. "Hop on," he said, handing me a helmet and making clear that his expectation was that I would ride on the back of his motorcycle. I climbed on and wrapped my arms around his waist.

Once I talked myself out of thinking there was anything unusual about riding on a motorcycle with your boss—maybe it was a normal "southern thing," I told myself—it was fun. He drove us on back roads surrounded by fields of cotton and corn and fruit orchards. I had never been on a motorcycle, and it was thrilling. We spent about an hour speaking with an elderly Black couple who owned a small farm outside town. They were generous enough to share their experiences of growing up in the Jim Crow South, and I absorbed everything they said. It was clear that they liked and trusted Morris. I could see why he had been so successful at building such an impactful organization against all odds and gaining the trust of the Black community in Montgomery.

We said our goodbyes and climbed back on the motorcycle. As we meandered along the back roads, I didn't recognize the route. It wasn't until we were heading down a dirt road that I realized we were not going back to my apartment.

We stopped by a river and Morris told me that he had packed us lunch and wanted to show me his favorite picnic spot. "Okay," I said, still trying to convince myself that this was normal. But when he started to undress, my mind started to race. "The best spot on the river is over there," he said, pointing to a spit of land on the other side of the river. "Don't worry, I'll carry the lunch basket. Come on."

By now he was completely naked in front of me. He hesitated for a moment, then waded into the river, picnic basket held high as he made his way to the other side. I don't remember what I was thinking or how I decided to do what I did next, but I picked a strategy and went with it.

I threw myself into the river—fully clothed, including my sneakers—and began swimming toward him as if there were nothing strange about it. I swam through the water, my pants, shirt, and shoes weighing me down, until I reached the riverbank. I pulled myself up and out of the water.

Morris was on a flat rock—still naked—and reached his arm out to offer me a sandwich. I took it and found a dry rock to sit on, pulling my knees up to my chin and averting my gaze. I don't remember what conversation we filled the time with. I only remember thinking that if I kept talking and acting as if everything were normal, I would get through this and back home.

Looking back, of course, it was the fine line that smart, powerful men walk when they don't want to get caught abusing their authority and power. They create a kind of plausible deniability. They don't demand anything from you. They don't force you. Rather, they create an environment where you are trapped. You understand what is expected of you, even if it is never articulated. They bank on your compliance, and later they call it consent.

At some point, Morris realized that I wasn't about to take my clothes off or comply. We headed back across the river and got on his motorcycle. When we arrived at my apartment, I jumped off and thanked him for a great afternoon—a tribute to my masterful ability to compartmentalize.

I walked up the path to my apartment, went in, locked the door, and took my first deep breath of the afternoon. That night, I lay in bed trying to make sense of what had happened. Despite having avoided what was supposed to be inevitable, I felt uneasy.

I wasn't traumatized as much as I was confused and concerned. I worried that my career would be negatively impacted before it began. After all, law students depend on strong recommendations to help them get the jobs they want upon graduation. I was scared that he would ask me to join him again and that when I said no,

I would be marginalized or even fired. I felt alone and unsure about what to do. I even began to question whether I was making something out of nothing. After all, wasn't I the college student who skinny-dipped with faculty and students at Strawberry Creek College and even had a romance with a graduate student instructor?

On Monday morning, I returned to work having decided not to tell anyone what happened. There were no women attorneys or supervisors in the office back then. The few women who were there worked in administrative roles, so when one of them asked me how my weekend went, I responded that it was fine and that I went on an investigation with Morris. Without missing a beat, she said: "Oh no, we were going to warn you about that. We didn't think it would happen so soon."

My experience wasn't a one-off. He had a pattern, and everyone knew and tolerated it. And with that, all my fantasies about social justice and movement lawyers creating spaces and organizations where women could also thrive and be respected went up in smoke.

Perhaps I should have seen it coming. After all, the women I knew in law school often shared their experiences with sexism in the profession—inappropriate comments made by professors, uncomfortable job interviews with potential male employers, or the pressure to "just have a drink" with the law firm partner. But I thought it would be different in my world of social justice lawyering. After all, if men who fought day in and day out for justice couldn't be trusted to behave around women, who could?

The experience with Morris taught me that just as demonizing people and reducing them to their worst moment obscures the full picture of their humanity, so does putting someone on a pedestal. It was a hard lesson. I realized that if I was going to find a nurturing and supportive haven for women in this profession, I was going to have to create it myself.

———

My summer ended in the last place you would expect to find a Jewish woman: a Ku Klux Klan rally.

I was assigned to assist a group of lawyers and investigators who were working to stop the KKK from terrorizing Black communities. The team was using litigation to challenge the KKK, so they needed to collect as much information as possible at local chapters. When they suggested that I accompany one of the investigators to a Klan rally to gather evidence, I thought they were joking. They were not, and days later I found myself in a car heading to a small town in southern Georgia where a KKK rally was set to start at sundown.

Our assignment was simple: observe, listen, and take photos of participants and license plates. We approached the grassy field where the rally was happening. I was filled with trepidation. I looked around and was surprised to see families sitting on brightly colored blankets spread out casually as young children played noisily nearby. It had the feeling of a small summer festival or family reunion. There was barbecue, hot dogs, and sweet iced tea by the gallon. Conversation and laughter filled the air. The atmosphere was festive and light.

As we made our way around the crowd, my companion, Bruce, would start conversations with random people. There was nothing unusual about it. They talked about the things we all care about—children, weather, and aging parents.

There were moments when I had to remind myself of where I was. I stayed silent, fearing that my New York accent would expose me. My undercover outfit—a white T-shirt with a picture of a Klansman on a horse and the words INVISIBLE EMPIRE written across it—gave me a slight sense of security. But when Bruce would nudge me to stand next to different participants, pretending to take a picture of me, "his wife," he was actually building a database of Klan members in the local town. I was sure that I would be discovered. It was exciting and terrifying.

As night fell, the speakers took the stage. There were the predictable rants about Black people, Jews, and immigrants. It was hateful, but the absurdity of the claims somehow reduced my fear. It was hard to take seriously someone who claimed that people in town were developing cancer because "Yankee Jews" were putting poison in the water.

Couldn't we solve this problem with education and accurate, reliable sources of information? I thought to myself, perhaps naively. Couldn't more proximity to the people you hate upend the false narratives? Just as I was contemplating these simple answers to an age-old problem, everyone was asked to join hands around the huge wooden cross on the hill. Now many of the people who moments ago had been eating hot dogs and laughing with their children donned white robes and hoods. The cross was set on fire, and it all became very real very quickly, and the fear that I had pushed away all night began to overwhelm me.

Until that moment, the ability to engage with people at the rally one on one had given me solace and even some amount of hope. People whom I could hate, and who surely hated me, or at least my Jewish identity, transformed once I engaged with them.

One on one, there always seemed to be the possibility of changing a heart or mind. But as always, this fades quickly when groupthink sets in. When the world is suddenly divided into "us" and "them" and fear takes root, people will say and do the worst things to others. As I watched the cross burn, lighting up the night sky on that desolate hill, I grappled with one question.

If it came down to it, would I defend any of these people the same way that I would defend the young Black man who was facing death or the women at Bedford Hills? Would I be able to see past their hate and find the human being who was still worthy of dignity and capable of redemption?

My mind raced for loopholes, but my heart answered very clearly: yes.

Years later, I would defend people who would send me straight back to that night, wondering if I had chosen right.

5

Defeat versus Resilience

Perhaps I'm not made for this. I remember the first time I had that thought. It came four years into my career as a public defender. My client's name was Martin.

I remember walking into the dingy, small cement jail cell where he was waiting. He was seated behind a small metal table, hands clasped in front of him, nervously looking around.

I sat down and looked across the table at a man who could have been my family member. He was Jewish and had emigrated from Russia with his mother. He was ten years my senior, had a college degree, and worked as an architect. He had a trace of a Russian accent but spoke softly, clearly, and with impeccable

English. I introduced myself and opened the file that had the charges against him.

"Do you know what you are being charged with?"

He nodded.

"Okay, then, I need to ask you some questions about yourself and then about the charges against you. This is so that I can prepare the best defense possible and try to get bail set in an amount you can pay. Anything we talk about is completely confidential."

Martin was charged with sodomy in the first degree—a class B felony that carried the possibility of up to twenty-five years in state prison. The charging document did not specify a particular date that the alleged crime occurred; rather it stated that "on or about" a specified month, the "defendant put his penis in the anus of Alan, a boy 9 years old."

In the inevitable hierarchy of charges that bring on the most outrage in those inside and outside the system, top of the list is any offense involving a child, particularly when there is an allegation of a sexual offense.

It's an understandable reaction. But as a public defender, I had to train myself to suspend judgment, be curious about the larger context, and stay open to seeing the whole person.

Martin responded to my questions with cursory, monotone answers. He displayed no emotion and simply stated that he didn't do "that" and had no idea why the boy was saying it.

The boy was Martin's nephew, his sister's son. His sister had recently divorced the boy's father, a police officer.

When Martin was arraigned in court later that day, the prosecutor read the charges out loud. I saw the disgust on the faces of the court officers and court personnel. The presumption of innocence is the foundation of our legal system, but as a public defender I have seen too many times when a person is presumed guilty the minute the cuffs go on. In those moments, I always feel the need to reassure my client with a gentle touch to let them know I'm there, I still see them as a person, they are not alone, and I still presume their innocence. To dispel any myths, defense attorneys rarely, if ever, ask our clients, "Did you do it?" because in our system the burden of proof is on the prosecution to prove guilt with credible and objective facts. The responsibility of the defense attorney is to defend their client.

In New York, the prosecutor is required to give defense counsel notice of any statements made by the accused to law enforcement. So at Martin's arraignment, the prosecutor—pausing for dramatic effect and then raising her voice with indignation—announced that "the defendant stated to the police officer, 'I only kissed his penis.'"

It felt like a gut punch. It's never good to hear that your client confessed. It's a huge hurdle to undo with juries. Most people refuse to believe that someone would confess to something that they didn't do, even when there is science and ample evidence to the contrary. It is unimaginable, if you haven't experienced the terror of being in an interrogation room. We all like to think that nothing could make us confess to something we didn't do. However, in my experience, make someone afraid enough and dangle the possibility of lessening their suffering, and they will often say whatever it takes to get to safety.

I've never been incarcerated. I've always been a visitor. But my first few years as a public defender were plagued with regular panic attacks when I visited clients in jail. The clank of the metal door closing behind me, locking me into the attorney-client visiting cell, often made me feel like my throat was closing and I couldn't breathe. My hands would get clammy, my breathing irregular, and my heart would pound as if it were about to explode. I often worried that I would pass out, or even die, before anyone noticed. Of course, it was completely self-generated. I was never in danger of losing my liberty or my life. But the panic and fear that would set in once I lost control over my body—even for an hour—gave me a tiny glimpse into what it might feel like to lose my freedom to incarceration. I have never forgotten this feeling.

The prosecutor indicated that Martin's confession was verbal, meaning there was no signed statement. It was going to be the police officer's word against that of Martin, who denied ever making such a statement. But something felt off. The charge against Martin was for anal sodomy, but his confession said he only kissed the boy's penis. Why would he confess to one thing, then be charged with something different? As those who have worked in the criminal system well know, these cases are complicated, but still, it was enough to raise a flag.

The judge set bail at $10,000 and ordered the case put over for the grand jury. A bail that high would have been impossible for almost every client I ever represented. Fortunately, Martin was able to call on his mother. She paid it and he was free.

Over the next few months, I did what lawyers do. I filed motions, conducted an investigation, and met with Martin frequently. Our relationship grew, and I could tell that he was beginning to trust me. Time after time Martin proclaimed his innocence and denied that he ever confessed anything to the police. In other words, he was saying the cops were making it up. The problem was, there was no way I could prove that.

From the outset, this case was riddled with reasonable doubts. There was no medical evidence of sexual assault. There were no witnesses. The crime wasn't reported for months. It was going to boil down to the word of his nephew and Martin's alleged confession to the police. And I had to convince a jury that one was a lie and the other was fabricated.

So why on earth would a child concoct a story like this about his uncle? I knew that's what a jury would be thinking, so it was my job as Martin's defender to provide an answer.

Here, the child was caught in the middle of a terrible divorce. And when he was at his father's house, it was revealed, he witnessed his father having sex with his young girlfriends. In addition, there were pornographic magazines left out and pornography was often on the television. Even though it was impossible to know for sure whether his exposure to sexually explicit materials, coupled with his parents' nasty divorce, had led Alan to make his claim about Martin, it was certainly a plausible explanation.

Public defenders don't always know what really happened in

a client's case. While we would prefer to know "the truth," it isn't essential to doing the job. Think about it this way: The prosecutor builds the house (the case against the accused), but it is only the defender who tests the strength of the house, beam by beam, finding the vulnerabilities and weaknesses of the structure. Can this house stand, or will it collapse? The weaknesses are the "reasonable doubts" that call into question the legitimacy of the government's case against the accused. Find just one, and a jury must acquit (in theory).

Having landed on a credible explanation for why Alan would make up the story, I still had to convince the jury that the confession never happened. In our system, pretrial hearings are held to determine whether or not the accused was properly given their *Miranda* warnings by the officer and whether or not the confession/statement was given freely. Watching *Law & Order* might lead you to think that false confessions and bad evidence routinely get thrown out of court, but nothing could be further from the truth. It almost never happens. Very few cases ever go to hearings, and even fewer cases make it to trial (fewer than 3 percent).[1] The entire system relies on guilty pleas. That means that police conduct is rarely examined or challenged in a courtroom. And cops and prosecutors both know it.

As I prepared for Martin's upcoming hearing, I knew the odds were against us, but I was determined to win. On the eve of the hearing, I was in my apartment cooking dinner when the doorbell rang. I wasn't expecting anyone and was annoyed at being disturbed when I had a long night of trial preparation ahead of me. When I opened the door, I was surprised to see Martin.

We had met before in my neighborhood, usually when I didn't have time during the week to meet and we used the weekends to prepare, but he never just appeared without notice, and never on my doorstep. He handed me a sealed yellow envelope with no writing on it. "Here," he said. "This is for you."

"What is it?" I asked.

"Just listen to it." And with that, he turned and walked down the block.

I couldn't imagine what was in the envelope. Maybe it was just a list of questions that he wanted me to ask at the hearing, or some information he wanted me to remember. Curious, I opened the envelope and found a cassette tape.

I had no idea why Martin would be giving me a tape on the eve of his hearing, but I dropped it in the cassette deck and resumed cooking dinner. At first, I couldn't figure out what I was hearing. I could make out men's voices, rising and falling in volume and tone, but I couldn't understand what they were saying. Then, suddenly, I realized what I was listening to. It was the interrogation. I froze, not wanting to miss a single word. I had never witnessed a real police interrogation. Lawyers and the public at large are almost never privy to what goes on in those rooms. As I listened, I realized why not.

The officers questioning Martin used every tactic they could to get him to confess, even threatening to kill him and "float him down a river, facedown." They cursed at him and pounded the table. I could imagine Martin in that room, alone, head down, praying for it to stop. Despite the pressure and the threats to kill him if he didn't tell them what they wanted to hear, Martin denied that he did anything. Over and over again, he denied the allegations. By the end of the tape, I realized that Martin had *never* said what the police alleged he had said.

The confession was a complete police fabrication.

I shouldn't have been shocked. I had heard countless stories from my clients about police interrogations. And I knew that the police pressure people in all sorts of ways—legal and illegal—to confess. This was worse. They didn't succeed in getting Martin to give a false confession; he never confessed at all!

Most of us have heard about the fog of war, where soldiers can make immoral decisions when clouded by the chaos of combat. This is something similar. Hell-bent on "getting the bad guy," police officers can ignore exculpatory evidence or, worse, build a case based on false or exaggerated evidence. In Martin's case, it seemed, the cops were unable to get a confession even under extreme pressure, so they simply made one up.

The idea that the police would invent a confession was unnerving. If Martin hadn't secretly taped the interrogation by wearing a hidden wire, and had the police not let him walk out of the precinct that afternoon, I probably would have believed that he made the confession. It doesn't mean that I would have believed the truth of his statement—false confessions happen—

but surely I would have believed he said *something*.[2] This was different.

Over the years, many of my clients had claimed that evidence was planted or invented by the police. Here, for the first time, I had proof not only of the inexcusable tactics but that such a level of dishonesty was possible.

The question was now one of strategy. I knew this recording would be an explosive revelation. I had to decide how to use it for maximum impact. The rules of discovery required me to share the tape with the prosecution only if I intended to introduce it into evidence at trial. However, if the purpose was only to use it for cross-examination of their witness, I was allowed to hold it back until the trial, allowing me to lock the cop into his lie at the pretrial hearing and later use his own testimony against him. I was thrilled but also worried about overplaying my hand. After all, I was still a fairly new public defender.

I spent the rest of the night listening carefully to the tape of the interrogation, taking notes, and preparing for the hearing the next day. When I arrived in the office early the next morning, bleary-eyed from the long night before, I confided in one of my most trusted colleagues.

The idealist in me wanted to believe that the system operated to right wrongs, seek justice, and protect the accused. I should have been able to give the tape to the prosecutor and the judge and trust that the case would be thrown out. Unfortunately, even after only four years on the job, experience had taught me otherwise.

If I did disclose the tape, they would find a way not to use the statement at trial and still move forward against Martin, relying on the boy's testimony. The only hope I had to convince a jury that the entire case was a fabrication was to prove, before their eyes in real time, that the statement being admitted into evidence by the prosecution was a complete invention by the police. It would create reasonable doubt and cast the entire prosecution in a questionable light.

We began the hearing shortly before 11:00 a.m. The prosecutor called their first and only witness to the stand. It was the police officer who ran the interrogation.

Sitting at the defense table with Martin, I turned to see the officer, in plain clothes, confidently stride into the courtroom. He took the witness stand, put one hand on the Bible, raised his other hand in the air, and swore to "tell the truth, the whole truth, and nothing but the truth."

For the next thirty minutes the prosecutor asked questions of the officer about the circumstances of Martin's confession. I had heard questions like these asked hundreds of times to countless police officers. And I had heard the same rote answers.

"Officer, did you use any threats to make Mr. Rosenberg confess?"

"No, Counselor, I did not," he responded.

"Officer, did you read Mr. Rosenberg his *Miranda* warnings?"

"Yes, Counselor, I did."

"And did he waive his right to remain silent?"

"Yes, Counselor, he did."

"And what, if anything, did Mr. Rosenberg tell you about the incident?"

"He stated that he 'only kissed his penis.'"

"Did he say anything else, Officer?"

"No, Counselor, that was his only statement."

"Thank you, Officer. Your Honor, we have no further questions of this witness."

The judge looked my way. "Counselor, do you wish to question the witness?"

"Yes, I do," I said, rising from my chair.

I walked slowly to the podium in the middle of the room, so that I was standing directly in front of the witness. As I looked him in the face, I was so angry that it felt physical. I took a breath and reminded myself to stick to the game plan.

The night before, I had meticulously written down what the police officer had said to Martin during the interrogation. Now it was time to confront him with his own words. I started slowly. "Officer, you just told this court that you never made any threats to Mr. Rosenberg. Is that correct?"

"Yes, Counselor, that is correct." And I was off to the races.

Question after question, I repeated the words I had heard on that tape with precision. "So, Officer, you never said to Mr. Rosenberg, 'I'm going to make sure that your body floats down a river, facedown, when you are dead'?"

"Absolutely not, Counselor," he said, staring me directly in the eyes.

"And you never said, 'I'll fucking kill you,' to Mr. Rosenberg?"

Now he was smiling at me. He assumed that I was just relying on what Martin had told me about the interrogation. He knew that no one would believe it, so he continued.

"No, Counselor, I did not say that. I would *never* use language like that." The smirk on his face made me want to pull the tape right then and there, but I knew I had to be patient, stay cool, and lock him into his answers, so that when the trial started, I could expose his corrupt lies. Martin, who was fully aware of my strategy, sat quietly at the defense table.

Unsurprisingly, the judge ruled that the confession was given voluntarily and after *Miranda* warnings had been administered, so it could be admitted as evidence. I had laid the trap for the officer. Now I just had to execute on my strategy.

The morning the trial began, I put on my most conservative trial clothes. Juries are keen observers of trial lawyers. They notice everything—how you dress, how you react when a witness says something, how you interact with your client, how the judge reacts to you, and even whom you acknowledge in the audience.

As I was leaving the house, I worried that the jury would think I was a naive, single young woman or, worse, someone who didn't care about the welfare of children. Reaching into my jewelry box, I pulled out a ring that had been my mother's wedding ring and slipped it on my left ring finger. Better for Martin if the jury thought I was married and might have children (hey, prosecutors have their tricks, defenders have ours).

Jury selection went as expected. Many potential jurors, when hearing the nature of the charges against Martin, told the judge that they couldn't be fair to the defense and were excused. It may be that jurors who express concern about their ability to be fair are precisely the jurors you might want, because they are at least thoughtful about their role, biases, and responsibilities. However, once they express those doubts, they are excused from service. It's the juror who is hiding their disgust or bias against your client that you have to worry about. We had a jury by the end of the week.

As predicted, the case boiled down to two witnesses—Alan, Martin's nephew, and the police officer who interrogated Martin.

When Alan walked into the courtroom, my heart sank. He was adorable. He was not old enough to be sworn in and take an oath to tell the truth, so the only way he would be allowed to testify was if the judge determined, after questioning him, that he had a sufficient understanding of what it means to tell the truth and what it means to lie. It's a strangely quiet, intimate process, and it takes place outside the presence of the jury.

Alan climbed up into the witness box. Once seated, he was barely big enough to see. He had a stuffed animal in his lap—a dog with floppy ears—that he clung to as the judge softly asked him questions. After about fifteen minutes of gentle questioning, the judge determined that Alan had a sufficient understanding of what truth is and ruled that he would be allowed to testify as an unsworn witness. With that, the boy climbed out of the witness box, doggy in hand, and walked right by our defense table without looking at me or Martin.

Once he was out of the courtroom, I rose to my feet. "Judge, I have a request."

"Yes, Counselor. What is it?"

I took a deep breath. "Judge, now that you have ruled that Alan can testify, I am going to ask you to instruct him that he may not hold his stuffed puppy on his lap while testifying. As much as I understand it might be comforting for him to do so, it is prejudicial to my client. I am asking you to remove the puppy from his lap while he testifies."

There are moments in a defense lawyer's career when you realize that you are the most hated person in the courtroom. Sometimes it's because of whom you represent. Or what your client is charged with. Sometimes your tactics or strategy offends observers, even if completely justified. This was definitely one of those moments. The prosecutor and court personnel stared in disbelief.

In their eyes, I was now the monster. The judge, whose wide face started to turn red, was incredulous. "Really?" he said.

"Yes, Judge. Really." I stayed focused. "Judge, I wouldn't ask if I didn't think it would have a prejudicial effect on my client. You might as well have him testify with a halo over his head. The jury will have to assess whether or not they think this young boy is telling the truth. Doing that while he clings to a stuffed puppy might influence them, and so I am asking you to remove it."

I could see that the judge was trying to regain his composure. I knew that he didn't want to do it, so I was surprised when he ruled in my favor—no puppy on the lap while testifying.

We did our opening statements. Predictably, the prosecutor's opening was hard-hitting—her outrage clear. My opening statement was nothing short of pleading with the jury just to keep an open mind and listen carefully to the witnesses.

I had to hold back what I had—clear evidence that there was a police conspiracy to frame Martin for this crime—or the police officer and prosecutor would be tipped off and given the opportunity to try to explain away the unforgivable. I sat down and waited. The prosecutor called to the stand the police officer who interrogated Martin and whom I had cross-examined at the pretrial hearing days earlier. His testimony was locked in. There was no escape. I just had to be patient and let him dig himself in deeper.

Then it was my turn. "Counselor, do you wish to cross-examine this witness?"

"Yes, Judge, I most certainly do."

I stood up, gathered my notes, and grabbed a cassette player from my briefcase. I walked to the podium and arranged my files—leaving the cassette player in plain view. I could see that the judge was perplexed, but he didn't say anything. I began my questioning, slowly and methodically, committing him to his answers.

"So you never cursed at Mr. Rosenberg?" I asked.

"No, Counselor."

"You are absolutely sure of that, Officer?"

"Yes, Counselor, I am sure."

"And you *never* threatened his life?" Now our eyes were locked.

"Absolutely not, Counselor. I would never do such a thing."

We did the same dance from the earlier hearing. He had no idea what was coming. I marveled at his arrogance. His complete confidence that there was nothing I could do to prove that he had lied. In any other circumstance, he could have depended on the fact that it is almost always impossible to prove that a police officer is lying. In fact, lying is so common that around the court-house it's called police "testilying." But here, for once, I had the goods.

After locking the officer into his answers, giving him no room to change his story, it was time. "Officer, I am going to play you something. Could you tell me whether or not you recognize the first voice on this tape?" I pushed play.

The voice on the tape was clearly the officer's. The tape ran for only about ten seconds before the judge stopped the proceed-ing and ordered me up to the bench.

"Robin, what is that?"

"Judge, it's a tape that I plan to use to cross-examine this of-ficer with," I said calmly. The prosecutor still hadn't caught on, but the judge was onto me.

"Counselor, I said, *What is that?* What is that a recording of?"

I hesitated, calculating what to say. "Judge, it's a tape of the questioning of Mr. Rosenberg by this officer." Now they knew. Without missing a beat, the judge excused the police officer from the witness box, sent the jury into the jury room for a recess, and ordered me and the prosecutor into his chambers. For the next hour, chaos ensued.

The prosecutor, who finally realized the magnitude of what

was happening, objected to my using the tape. She had no legal grounds for the objection, but that didn't stop her. She used what I call the "But Judge, it will hurt my case" objection. It is surprisingly effective when deployed by the prosecution.

The judge advised the prosecutor to find the police officer a lawyer right away. Shockingly, the judge seemed more concerned with the police officer's legal jeopardy than with the irrefutable evidence that the officer had committed perjury in his courtroom. I thought I had joined a system that was designed to protect the accused—my client. But in practice, the system was organizing to protect a corrupt police officer whose guilt was undeniable.

Naively, I had thought that once the judge realized that the "confession" was a police fabrication, he would be outraged and right the wrong, declaring the entire prosecution of Martin a gross injustice. I had dreamed that the judge would stop at nothing to preserve the integrity of his courtroom, his profession, and the so-called halls of justice he was a part of. I had even fantasized that he would order the prosecutor to conduct a criminal investigation of the wrongdoing. Sometimes hope springs eternal.

The judge left his desk, leaving me and the prosecutor in his chambers. We didn't speak. I clutched the tape in my hand. When he returned, he announced that he wouldn't let me use the tape for cross-examination until it was "authenticated." Since that was precisely what I had been doing when I asked the police officer if he recognized the voice on the tape, I thought we were heading back into the courtroom for me to continue the cross-examination.

"Ms. Steinberg, give the tape to the prosecutor so she can have it authenticated." Before I had a moment to think, I responded. "Judge, there is no way that I will give this tape to anyone. It is not leaving my possession."

He stared at me, weighing what to do next. "If I order you to turn it over, you will turn it over," he insisted. "No, Judge, I will not." I knew that my refusal to comply with the order could land me in jail, cited for contempt. Now blood was rushing to my face and my ears were ringing. The lines were drawn. I was in way over my head, and I knew it. I didn't know what was going to happen next.

"Robin, I am not going to let you use it unless you can prove to me that it is authentic and has not been tampered with or altered in anyway." It was a close call. The judge decided to let me keep the tape, but now I had to figure out a way to get it independently authenticated so that I could use it. Without that, we were sunk.

The next morning, I hopped on a plane to Washington, DC, cassette tape tucked into my jacket pocket, and headed to an FBI office in Virginia, where an agent had agreed to check the tape for any alterations or tampering.

The night before I left, I looked Martin in the eyes and asked him one last time: "Martin, you didn't do anything to change this tape, right?" He assured me that he had not.

The judge had agreed to put the trial over for forty-eight hours to allow me to make the trip. I dropped the tape off and went back to my hotel room to continue preparing for the trial. The next day, the agent called me. "Well, I have good news and bad news," he said. I braced myself. "The bad news is that the tape has been spliced. Someone removed a piece of the tape. I don't know what was on it, but it's missing. The good news is that other than that one section, the tape is authentic and hasn't been tampered with. Good luck, Counselor." And with that, my defense was gone.

By the time I got back to New York City, it was early evening. I tried to push out of my mind all the things I wanted to say to Martin, and all the things that I was sure the prosecutor and judge would say to me in court the next day. I needed to focus, pivot my strategy, and mount a strong defense if we were to have a fighting chance.

The doorbell rang. It was Martin. All things considered, I was stunned that he had the nerve to show up. "Martin, I don't have time right now. I have to figure out what our defense is going to be now that we can't use the tape." Martin lifted his arm, handing me an envelope. "Here, please listen," he said.

"Good night, Martin. I'll see you in court tomorrow." These are the moments when compartmentalizing reality comes in handy. I didn't say anything and turned to go back into the apartment.

I popped the new cassette tape into my machine and listened. At first, I thought it was the identical tape and had no idea why Martin had brought it to me. I could hear the officer threatening him and I could hear his repeated and plain denials of guilt.

I was about to turn the machine off when, suddenly, I heard Martin say something about his mother. I knew the tape inside and out and didn't remember any mention of his mother. But there—clear as a bell—I could hear Martin lose his composure and call his mother a "bitch." Every single other thing about the tape was identical to the original that I had submitted to the FBI. It was clear now. Martin had tampered with the tape not to protect himself but to avoid having anyone hear him say something bad about his mother. As mad as I was that my defense was torpedoed, Martin's instinct strangely touched me.

The next morning, I marched into court. The judge already knew from the FBI agent that the tape had been altered, so when I started talking about a second tape—the unaltered one—he shut me down. He wasn't hearing any of it and ordered me to proceed with the trial.

"Judge," I implored him, "I will continue with the trial, but if I send someone else from my office, and they can get this new tape authenticated, will you let me use it?" He agreed but would not give me another minute and ordered the trial to continue.

One of the best things about being a public defender is working with other public defenders. We are an unusual crowd. We have our own language, steadfast devotion to clients, and a healthy dose of irreverence that often shows up as humor. We are bound together in a system where all the odds are against us and our clients. Sometimes you feel like you are in a bunker fighting oppositional forces, and the only support you have is your fellow public defender. Unlike my own family, my chosen public defender family would always show up when I needed them. And so one of my colleagues agreed to fly that night to Washington to authenticate the tape with the FBI.

Since we would have to wait for the FBI to confirm the tape's authenticity, the prosecutor didn't put the police officer back on the stand—that would have to wait for another day—so she called the boy to the stand.

The judge had agreed to allow the stuffed puppy to be under the witness chair, so that Alan knew it was there while he testified. Before he entered the courtroom, the court officer carefully placed the white-and-brown dog with the floppy ears under the chair and out of the jury's view.

When the prosecutor stood and announced that her next witness was Alan, the jury turned toward the back of the courtroom. Alan was led in by another member of the prosecutor's office, and we all watched as he made his way to the front of the courtroom and climbed into the witness box. I could see how uncomfortable the judge was. I spun the gold wedding ring on my finger.

The prosecutor gently started: "Good morning, Alan. Can you please tell the jury your whole name?" And with that very first question, Alan reached down and pulled up the secreted stuffed puppy with the floppy ears from underneath his chair and placed it directly on his lap, arms wrapped tightly around it. The judge looked down at me, as if daring me to say something, but I knew better than object in front of the jury. I had to accept defeat—the puppy had won.

Alan's testimony was straightforward. He described what allegedly happened to him in simple, unemotional tones: "He humped me." It was my turn to cross-examine him. I needed to establish the trauma of the divorce and his being exposed at that

THE COURAGE OF COMPASSION

age to pornography and his father's sex life. The jury had to understand how a boy so young could describe sexual acts the way he did and how his claim about Martin might have been a cry for attention during a traumatic time.

There are no *Perry Mason* moments in real defense work. No matter how skilled a cross-examiner you are, witnesses don't crack suddenly and admit they are making it up. Often, the best you can do is cross-examine a witness about the circumstances surrounding the alleged crime, with the hope that you can expose the implausibility of what they are saying or the reason that they might fabricate a story. With a child, this is a particularly delicate performance. I did the best I could to highlight the turmoil in this young boy's life at the time he made the claim about Martin. I knew it was a heavy lift, but with the tape, we had a fighting chance.

As I expected, the FBI authenticated the second tape. The officer was notified to return to the courthouse for his testimony. As I waited in the hallway for Martin to arrive that morning, I saw the officer. I said nothing and tried to walk past him. He took two steps, blocking my way, never breaking his angry gaze at me. He meant to intimidate me, and I was certainly afraid, but I had learned a long time ago to never let them see my fear.

"Move out of my way," I said in a calm but firm voice.

"I'll see you again, Counselor," he said, and stepped aside. I was sure that he didn't mean inside the courtroom.

When I stepped into the safety of the courtroom, I saw a small group of people huddled up at the bench. I didn't recognize the two men in gray suits speaking to the judge. The prosecutor was up there too, but she was standing back as the men spoke. When the judge noticed me, he looked up and ended the private conversation. "Good morning, Counselor," he said. The men in gray stepped back and away from the bench. The judge informed me that he was going to do an inquiry of the police officer before calling back the jury. I objected, but no one cared. I had done the unthinkable. A police officer's job, future, and potential freedom were on the line. Everyone knew it, and they were closing ranks to protect him.

My blood boiled as I watched him saunter into the courtroom buoyed by the knowledge that the system was designed to give him impunity. He sat down in the witness box with a faint smirk and swore to tell the truth and nothing but the truth.

The judge asked him if he had had enough time to speak to his lawyers. He said that he had. The judge then asked him if he was prepared to move forward with the questioning. He looked directly at me without a trace of regret or fear. "Your Honor, I will be asserting my Fifth Amendment rights against self-incrimination." And there it was. He was "lawyered up."

The police union supplied him with lawyers to protect him, and now he would refuse to answer any of my questions. There was no cross-examination to be had. And per the rules of discovery, because I had kept the tape for the sole purpose of cross-examination, I couldn't admit it as evidence. The tape was rendered useless. There was absolutely nothing I could do about it. The jury would never know that the so-called confession was a complete fabrication and that this officer was guilty of the crime of perjury. They would never hear the threats to shoot Martin or float him down the river. They would never know that law enforcement had decided to frame Martin. And they would never know that this mild-mannered man had bravely walked into a police station with a wire in his shirt and taped the interrogation.

The jury came back into the courtroom. The officer was already in the witness box. I asked him question after question, only to hear the same response. "I refuse to answer that question pursuant to my Fifth Amendment right against self-incrimination." After a while, I could see that the jury was tired of my questions and the officer's nonanswers. I had to stop, but I knew that the moment I sat down, the trial would be over. I was just delaying the inevitable.

The jury convicted Martin in only a couple of hours. He was taken into custody. A month later the judge sentenced him to five to fifteen years.

I tried to stop the sentence from being executed, filing motions with the appellate court, but it denied the motions and ordered him to start serving his sentence. I wrote him letters, promising that we would mount a rigorous appeal of his conviction, desperately trying to keep his spirits up and his hope for a successful appeal from fading.

Then one morning, as Martin sat in a cell in a maximum-security prison, I picked up the local paper over a cup of coffee. As I thumbed through the pages, my attention was drawn to a small photograph. It was a picture of the officer in Martin's case. For a moment, I thought he must have been fired, suspended, or, better yet, charged criminally with perjury. However, according to the article, the officer had *voluntarily* resigned from the police force in good standing. While Martin endured the trauma of prison for a crime that I never thought he did, the officer, whose crime was unequivocally captured on tape, would be off to an early retirement with pension and benefits paid by the taxpayers for the rest of his life.

It was a moment of complete and pure disillusionment. I was certain that if I had been a better lawyer, I would have been able to convince the jury that there was a reasonable doubt and Martin would not have been convicted. It was the first time I came close to walking away from public defense, deciding that it was too futile, too hard, and impossible to change the power balance. If I was unable to protect Martin, how could I be trusted with other clients' lives? If I couldn't expose a single officer with absolute proof of his criminality, how could I succeed in cases where we had only a client's word?

The years brought many of those. Accounts of beatings, threats, sexual victimization, and planted evidence. Stories that are hard to believe when you hear them once, until you hear them all the time. To the rest of the world, you seem paranoid and easily drawn to conspiracy thinking for believing your clients. But public defenders see how power truly operates in our society. We see the jungle behind the illusion of law and order.

We see how these rights and liberties we hold dear don't belong to everyone and are more fragile than you ever thought possible.

In truth, there is no "system." It is a group of human beings with egos, ambition, insecurities, and anger waging an unbalanced battle against another group of human beings who also have their own stories. The difference is one group can play by its own rules or even change the rules when convenient.

Martin remained in jail longer than I ever thought possible. His sentence of five to fifteen meant that he reached his first parole-eligible date five years after his conviction, but he was denied release.

Even though he had no prior criminal record and no disciplinary issues while in prison, the parole board denied him release because he refused to "accept responsibility" for a crime he resolutely denied committing.

He valiantly clung to his innocence, time after time, parole hearing after parole hearing, choosing to remain in prison rather than falsely admit guilt. Finally, ten years after his conviction, Martin reached his "conditional release" date, the point where two thirds of his maximum sentence had been completed and when the convicted is supposed to be released and placed on parole. But Martin wasn't released. His insistence on his innocence and refusal to participate in a sex offender program in prison meant that the system could keep him locked in a jail cell until the very last possible day—fifteen years after his conviction—and that is exactly what it did.

Maybe those Berkeley hippies were right after all. . . . Perhaps there was no way to fight for meaningful change within the palace walls.

History should remind us that the fundamental constitutional protections afforded everyone who faces a criminal accusation, like the right to be presumed innocent until *proven* guilty, or the requirement that guilt be proved beyond a reasonable doubt, are not legal technicalities. Rather, they are the guardrails that protect all of us. Nothing teaches you that lesson faster than when a person you love is accused of something and winds up in the criminal justice system. At that moment, even the most cynical become warriors for the Constitution and fierce defenders of the presumption of innocence.

The countless wrongful convictions and the lives destroyed by incarcerating innocent men and women time and time again should be enough of a cautionary tale about the dangers of closing ranks at the expense of what is right. It isn't just the "blue wall of silence" in police departments. Doctors can close ranks around other doctors who commit malpractice. Members of a political party can cover up for one another. Religious institutions can protect clergy who abuse children. We are all susceptible to it. We all fear being banished from a group.

Certainly, after the defeat in Martin's case, I could have walked away, but I knew that if I did, I would not be able to live with myself. It's precisely in those moments when things get hard that you have to dig deep, remember why you do what you do, and find the resilience to continue. Sometimes justice requires finding the courage to stand alone, but it doesn't mean you have to stop there. What I knew now was that I couldn't just return to the palace alone. It was time to build an army and take the palace by storm.

6

Knowing It versus Feeling It

Officer please don't shoot cause my hands up
My hands up, my hands up.

—*"Hands Up" by Leonard Grant, aka Uncle Murda*

The song "Hands Up" dropped on December 4, 2014, the day after a grand jury in New York decided not to indict the NYPD officers who had choked Eric Garner to death. The accompanying music video contained real-life footage of uniformed officers brutalizing Black men and women in cities across America. It also included fictional sequences, including a controversial scene where one of the Black musicians points a gun at a white police officer in an act of revenge fantasy.

Less than twenty-four hours after the song dropped, strangers called for my firing and my head. Meanwhile, my organization, the Bronx Defenders, became embroiled in controversy surrounding this video.

Two of our attorneys had appeared in a brief fictionalized scene where a grieving mother seeks legal help and they are seen consoling her. Though the scene was no more than a few seconds long, the outrage that our office had participated in the video at all was red-hot. It nearly ended our city contract, even though, at the time, our public defender office was well established. We had been going strong for eighteen years and serving more than thirty thousand Bronx residents annually, and then suddenly, we were on the brink.

It's amazing how easy it is to lose control of your story and become defined by a single moment in the eyes of society. It's a lesson that I had learned in my years representing people in criminal cases but one that would really hit home when—in an instant—my life's work and career were reduced to "lying lawyer who produced cop-killer video."

I founded the Bronx Defenders in 1997, a decade after Martin's trial. In the beginning, it was only eight of us: six public defenders, a social worker, and an investigator. Living in New York City, there was no proverbial garage to start our organization out of, so instead we burned the midnight oil and cast our dreams in a small, dingy office in the Grand Concourse Plaza between a Rent-A-Center and a RadioShack.

This was my idea of taking the palace by storm. I was going to build a new kind of public defender office and train a new generation of lawyers on how to put up a real fight, center our clients' voices, and think about our work through a systemic lens. In short:

we were going to redefine what it meant to do public defense in the first place.

Traditional public defense tends to focus on only the client's criminal case, missing the larger reality of how an arrest can up-end a person's life.

When you are arrested, the impact on your life does not stop with the criminal case. Even before you are found guilty or innocent, a cascade of "collateral consequences," as they are called in the literature, can follow. You can get evicted, have your children taken away, lose your immigration status. Clients would often tell me that they cared more about the risk of any of those things happening than even about going to jail.

Beginning in the 1990s, many states moved to expand these collateral consequences as a way of being "tougher" on crime. The impacts ranged from ineligibility for food stamps, public housing, and federal financial aid to being excluded from certain professions and losing hard-earned occupational licenses. Believe it or not, in some jurisdictions, a felony conviction can result in losing a barber's license. In some cases, states can bar the person from voting and even terminate parental rights. Today, over forty thousand such civil penalties exist in state and federal statutes.[1] They feed a vicious cycle. Poverty is a driver of crime, and the collateral consequences of a criminal record make it harder to escape poverty.

There are over ten million arrests every year in the United States, and most cases end in plea bargains.[2] More than 80 percent are for misdemeanors.[3] As many Americans have criminal records as have college degrees.[4] These records create structural barriers to economic mobility and stability, and the effects are disproportionate on communities of color, which are not only historically underserved and impoverished but also the targets of overpolicing.[5]

The South Bronx was a perfect example of this. It was and remains one of the poorest congressional districts in the country and one of the most overpoliced.[6]

In thinking about the organization that I wanted to start, I knew that to do right by this community, it wasn't going to be enough to offer free criminal defense. We had to think bigger and see how different legal systems, like the criminal and family courts, intersect to create a perfect storm in a person's life. If public defense was to be a real and trusted resource for the poor and play a lasting role in combating structural racism and economic inequality in our society at large, it would have to change.

But change is not always easy. Indeed, it's often not even welcome.

At the time, the large institutional provider of public defense in New York City was the Legal Aid Society, where I had once worked as a young public defender. It was a huge organization spanning all five boroughs, with a large bureaucracy, an entrenched hierarchy, and many legal divisions that employed its almost one thousand staff.

For decades, it was the only game in town for young lawyers who wanted to do public defense, so it housed some of the most brilliant trial lawyers in New York City, but it also sheltered many who had long lost their dedication to clients and their cause. The lawyers and support staff were unionized and clashed with management over working conditions, salary, and client representation issues. I was grateful to be working at Neighborhood Defender Service (NDS) in Harlem when, in 1994, the Legal Aid staff lawyers went on an ill-fated strike, only to quickly vote to return to work when the mayor at the time, Rudolph Giuliani, threatened to cancel Legal Aid's contract with the city. It was a hard lesson in understanding power and your enemy, but the hardest lesson was still to be learned.

Still furious about the walkout, the city announced the following year that it was putting out a request for proposals for the creation of new additional organizations that could provide representation for indigent New Yorkers in the criminal justice system in each borough. It was a flagrant and direct attack on the Legal Aid Society, taking away 20 percent of its work in each borough, and it created a political minefield for anyone who thought of getting involved.

I knew that, but I also knew it was an opportunity to start a new public defender office at scale and from scratch. By now, I had been a public defender for fifteen years, trained countless young lawyers, and helped grow and manage NDS. I knew I had the experience necessary to start a new organization, but did I have the guts to try? My friend and dedicated criminal defense attorney Dan Arshack tried to convince me that we could do it by putting together my experience as a public defender manager and his acumen as a private criminal defense lawyer with a head for business. I was intrigued but deeply conflicted.

One day, I sat down with my boss, then the director of NDS, Leonard Noisette, and we talked about the idea. NDS was going to submit a proposal in response to the RFP to expand and institutionalize its work in Manhattan. We both knew that the organization needed more funding and stability if it was going to sustain itself and continue to be a valuable resource to the Harlem community. Then came the question of whether I should submit a proposal, separate from NDS's, to create a new public defender office in the South Bronx.

If I was going to go out and start something new, I knew the South Bronx was where I had to be. Lenny, always thoughtful, generous, and supportive, gave me the green light to go ahead if I wanted. It was an endorsement that later cost him standing with some of his staff at NDS but one for which I will always be grateful.

Still worried about the political fallout of starting a new office, I reached out to Chris Stone. Chris was one of the smartest people I had ever met, and he knew the politics of indigent defense in New York City. He also knew me well and had supported my leadership long before I could see it myself.

Over lunch in a small diner downtown, Chris questioned me about my reluctance and concerns about throwing my hat in the ring. I talked about my concern that if dedicated defenders didn't stand up and create these new offices, the city contracts might go to well-entrenched private-bar lawyers with little regard for clients. As I saw it, the city was about to throw thousands and thousands of low-income people charged with crimes out the window, and the only question was who would step up to break the fall. Was standing on the sidelines for the sake of political solidarity with Legal Aid more important than the lives of the human beings who were going to hit the ground?

"This is so fraught because the whole thing comes from a horrendous attack on Legal Aid by the mayor," I complained. "Everyone will *hate* me if I do this." As the words tumbled out of my mouth, I was ashamed to realize that my reluctance was about me, not about what was best for people in the South Bronx.

Chris sat back in his chair, mildly annoyed at my immaturity. He looked me straight in the eye and delivered what I then thought was only personal advice. "Robin, if you want to do something impactful that really matters, some people are going to hate you. That's just the way it is. This is a chance to do something big and powerful. Stop worrying about what people will think."

I can't count the number of times that I have clung to those wise words over the course of my career. There is simply no way to make real change without bruising egos. You can navigate the terrain carefully, but once you challenge the way things have been done, entrenched interests will always push back. Sometimes it can be painful, especially when the attacks become personal, but knowing why you fight is the key to pushing forward and staying focused.

We won the contract, and on Labor Day of 1997, we opened

the doors of the Bronx Defenders. Our new office was founded on a simple promise: We would listen to our clients and fight tooth and nail for their rights and dignity. We would approach our representation by learning about the whole individual, not just the case assigned to us. Our goal wasn't just to be friendly and supportive to our clients. It was to be effective. In addition to fighting the criminal case, our goal was to represent these clients on issues of housing, child-removal proceedings, and immigration that could be triggered by a criminal prosecution. To mitigate those risks, we needed to have a holistic view of the client's situation. We needed holistic defense, as the model is now called.[7]

By the time "Hands Up" exploded in 2015, the Bronx Defenders was nationally recognized as the gold standard of public defense. Our office employed over three hundred public defenders and advocates, served over thirty thousand people annually, ran intensive trial skills programs attended by public, private, and even military lawyers, and had received a grant from the U.S. Department of Justice to train public defender offices nationwide on the principles and strategies of holistic defense.

It was a great success story but one that did not matter when we were accused of endorsing violence against police officers.

How did I land in such a mess around a rap video?

It's actually quite simple. Representatives for the two rappers, Leonard Grant (Uncle Murda) and Jermaine John Coleman (Maino), had approached the Bronx Defenders about creating a music video to highlight the trauma of police violence in Black communities. They asked if they could film a short scene in our office. As part of the story told in the video, they wanted to show a fictional grieving mother coming to our office to seek legal help. Even though this was not the type of thing we had ever done, it was an issue of deep importance to the community we served and to our office. With my endorsement, two of our attorneys agreed to participate. All in all, they appeared in about ten seconds of footage.

The musicians had agreed to let us see the final video where the footage would be used before publishing it, but after the Garner decision, they ended up releasing the video without showing us first.

It was after midnight when I got home from a demonstration for Eric Garner and saw the first email in my in-box. It was from the *New York Daily News*. The reporter asked about a rap video that "had the police unions upset" and whether we had any comment.

I suddenly realized our brief appearance had given the police unions the perfect ammunition to come after the Bronx Defenders and make the situation as damaging as possible. It did not matter that our office's involvement had been minimal. They had the perfect opportunity to try to take us down. After eighteen years of building the Bronx Defenders carefully and strategically, I felt naive and responsible for creating such a vulnerability. I should have seen how it could be weaponized. Even my college-age son, Jacob, showed better political instincts. "Mom . . . I get what these guys are doing and I know this issue is important, but c'mon, the guy goes by 'Uncle Murda.' . . . What exactly did you think the cops would do with that?"

The days that followed were a complete nightmare, from Greta Van Susteren on Fox News demanding that Mayor Bill de Blasio defund the Bronx Defenders—and that I be fired—to a former prosecutor suggesting that I be treated like a rattlesnake (read: cut off my head).

News trucks parked outside our office in the South Bronx at what seemed to be all hours of the day. Patrol cars drove around the block repeatedly, their sirens blaring. Cops took up the habit of following us randomly, including into a diner near my apartment, where an officer thought it would be amusing to bang his holstered gun into the side of my booth as I ate breakfast with a young colleague of mine.

Morale at the organization was low. In the courthouse up the street, judges, prosecutors, court officers, and public defenders from other agencies expressed outrage and dispensed daily doses of condemnation.

Solidarity was a rare commodity. Other social justice organizations expressed their sympathies in private, but none was willing to come out publicly in our defense. Harvard University, which was including me in a photo exhibit of women leaders as part of an International Women's Day tribute, withdrew the honor. The commercial bank that managed our payroll account dropped us as a client. No one wanted anything to do with us. Even my mother, who did not bother to watch the video, had the nerve to call me from California: "Robin, you are in the *LA Times*. How could you . . ."

Meanwhile, hate mail and death threats had become par for the course.

"Cop killers!" many of the letters read.

We had lost control of our narrative—to fight for the people in the South Bronx and take a stance on the issues that mattered to them—and now the organization we had built was at risk of collapsing. I wanted to fight back, but my board of directors was clear that I was to stand down and shut up. They were trying to protect us.

This wasn't the first time we had been reduced to a label. When we opened our doors in the late nineties, other attorneys called us "the Bronx Pretenders," and I was accused of being a "union buster" for launching our office in the aftermath of the failed strike at the Legal Aid Society. In those early days, the hostility in the courthouse was palpable. Judges questioned our competence in front of our clients, court personnel threw our case files on the floor when we weren't looking, and even within our own ranks of public defenders in New York, we were deemed outsiders and traitors.

One day, at the height of the "Hands Up" fiasco, I walked up to my assistant, Skylar, and said, "Hand them over." He froze. He knew I meant all the hate mail he had been hiding from me. "I know you've been keeping them from me. It's okay. I'm ready. I want to see them."

One by one, I opened the letters. Sitting alone in my office, with only a small desk lamp on, I read the letters late into the night. Some simply called for my resignation and admonished me to be ashamed of myself. Others reflected a kind of hatred and violence that shook me.

"How about a video called Fire Up the Ovens?" one of them said. "I hope that someday when the savages and n———s that you represent rape or try to murder you, that you have to call the police and they don't come."

No wonder Skylar had hidden them from me. I couldn't help but be scared. I tried to calm my mind and think my way through the terror. How would I ever regain my sense of security again? Would I always be looking over my shoulder? Would I have to move away, assume a new identity, and find a new career? There was only one way to find out.

I decided to reach out to every one of those strangers and try to begin a conversation. It may have been a crazy idea, but I knew that if I didn't face them directly, I would live in fear forever. In my mind I had an idea, a caricature of who these people were, but something inside me told me there was more to them. At least I hoped there was.

The first person I called, a former sheriff in a small town in Texas, answered the phone. "Hi," I said. "This is Robin Steinberg from New York City. You recently sent me a letter expressing how angry you are about my involvement in a video, so I thought I would call you directly and have a conversation about it. I really would like to understand why you are so mad. Would you be willing to share your thoughts with me?"

There was silence on the other end of the line, so I tried to encourage him. "I'm also happy to answer any questions you might have about why I did what I did," I said.

"No, that's okay. I don't have any questions," he said. He sounded tentative, even a little unsure, which gave me the confidence to continue. I explained that our involvement was minimal but that the video produced by the rappers was trying to bring to light the epidemic of police violence in Black communities in America, not encourage violence.

He responded by explaining that he had been a police officer for decades and that, in his experience, it was the police who had reasons to fear those same communities. He went on to talk about his colleague who had been shot and his own daily fear of not returning home at night to his wife and family. By the end of the conversation, we agreed that fear existed on both sides and that we could do better as a nation to bridge that gap. I thanked him for speaking with me and he apologized for the letter he had sent. I gave him my office number and encouraged him to call me anytime he wanted to talk again. He thanked me for the call.

I went on to respond to dozens more letters and emails. What I learned was that confronted with a real person, not the caricature they had formed in their mind, most of the senders were brought down to a space of civility. I learned the same lesson.

Before "Hands Up," the idea of sitting across the table from police officers gave me the chills. In my mind, I had collapsed them all into a single stereotyped "cop" who simply hated my clients and everything I stood for. In reality, many of these men and women in uniform were no older than my own children, and each had their own story and fears that shaped them. Institutions and systems can reinforce the "us versus them" mentality that leads us to dehumanize one another and close ranks at the expense of what is morally right, and can drive violent and racist behaviors. When we are in the fight, there is the fog of war, and we can't see the forest for the trees.

In the end, riding out the crisis came down to a plea bargain.

We had built the Bronx Defenders as an inside/outside player: an organization fighting for justice and equality while making the strategic decision to operate within the criminal justice system to hack away at its entrenched inner workings. We were the proverbial cog in the machine, except that this cog was purposefully off-kilter. It had been just a matter of time before the powers that be tried to hammer the cog into alignment, and this was it.

After a relentless news cycle, Mayor de Blasio issued a blistering statement condemning us, and the city's Department of Investigations (DOI) began an investigation. I couldn't help but appreciate the irony that when Eric Clapton sang "I Shot the Sheriff" on concert stages across America, no one took it literally. In fact, it became a number-one hit. Meanwhile, when two Black rappers frustrated with the world in which they lived portrayed a revenge fantasy within a music video, it was taken as an incitement to violence, not as an artistic expression, and the mayor of New York City was ready to defund public defense in the South Bronx.

Typically, the DOI investigates the misuse of public funds, so we willingly opened our financial books to demonstrate that no public funds had been used to produce the video. In fact, the two lawyers who participated in the scene had done so on their own time during a weekend. Our finances were impeccable, and the DOI knew it. Still, they went through the motions.

A DOI investigator, who was a former prosecutor, and his colleague came to my office for an interrogation. Once the niceties were over, he jumped right in. "Ms. Steinberg, did you see the lyrics to 'Hands Up'?" I told him the truth. I had briefly glanced at them but hadn't paid too much attention at the time. It was a minor request among a million priorities in an office representing thousands of people in four court systems. And remember, the video wasn't supposed to go up until we had a chance to review how the footage from our office would be used.

He took a sheet of 8½ × 11 white paper out of a folder, looked me straight in the eye, and ordered, "Read this out loud." I glanced down and saw the lyrics to "Hands Up" typed out on the paper. I'd been patronized enough in my lifetime by men like this, so I declined the invitation. "I will not," I said, handing the paper back to him. "How about we just agree that those are the lyrics to 'Hands Up'?" He took the paper back and, in a moment befitting a bad comedy, began to recite the lyrics out loud to me: "For Mike Brown and Sean Bell, a cop got killed. 'Cause I'm Black, police think they got the right to shoot me." He could not have made it clearer that he was enraged by the lyrics and ready to teach me a lesson.

In the end, my board suspended me without pay for two

months. It was a compromise with the mayor's office to secure the future of the organization while giving them something they could call a punishment. I couldn't help thinking about all the police officers who go on administrative leave with full pay after egregious misconduct. I didn't like it, but I took it in stride, knowing that the board had made the strategic decision to get out of harm's way as quickly as possible rather than fight about the merits of the accusations. It was an all-too-familiar bargain. Forgo truth for safety. I thought about all the clients I had stood next to over the course of my career who had pleaded guilty to something they did not do in exchange for the safety of going home, rather than risk losing everything if they went to trial to demand justice and truth. I swallowed my pride and took the suspension, promising my staff that I would be back.

We learn the most about ourselves and who our real friends are in the face of adversity. I call those few friends my lifeboat, and for the many people who came into our office for help, I wanted us to be precisely that: a lifeboat to safety.

After two months of exile, I returned to the Bronx Defenders more fired up than ever, with the same feeling of purpose I had felt three decades earlier when I stepped into my first courtroom. I was on a mission to leave the organization in the strongest position to continue to serve the people of the Bronx and challenge abuses of power. Unapologetically, I worked to reclaim our story and regain our footing.

It was only one year later, when Supreme Court justice Sonia

Sotomayor accepted our invitation to come to the Bronx Defenders for a public event with me, that I finally knew the organization was going to be all right. That night, as I sat in a big leather easy chair facing this extraordinary woman, I could finally exhale. We were back.

7

Judgment versus Curiosity

Baby Jordan was born HIV positive, with clubfeet and dwarfism. He couldn't sit up, crawl, or stand. His little body was delicate yet rigid, his limbs frozen in place. He had severe asthma that required constant vigilance and medical attention, and he was unable to communicate at all. Born to a drug-addicted mother, he was taken into foster care at birth. At eighteen months, it was a miracle he was still alive.

Faith Stevens loved him with all her heart. She had agreed to become his foster mother even though she was already raising two children on her own. Having two elementary school–age kids is a full-time job, but Faith could not say no to helping Jordan. And so, as mothers do, she found the extra energy and time to provide Jordan with everything he needed—nurturing him, administering oxygen, taking him to physical therapy, and never missing a day of the prescribed exercise regimen for him at home.

Faith had noticed that Jordan was crying more than usual, but she didn't understand why. Fortunately, he had a routine medical check coming up. When she took him for the exam, his pediatrician discovered that the baby was suffering from multiple fractures in his arms and legs. As a mandated reporter, the doctor immediately contacted the New York City Administration for Children's Services. In an instant, Faith went from heroic foster mother to criminal suspect.

Faith is a Black woman. The police wasted no time in arresting her. She was brought into the precinct and questioned for hours. Still in shock from the doctor's diagnosis, she swore that she was incapable of hurting a child, but no one believed her. How could a baby who wasn't able to crawl, walk, or move his arms and legs hurt himself? And wasn't he always under her watch? On the surface, every factor seemed to point to Faith, but the truth is always more complicated, and the presumption of innocence asks us to suspend judgment until all the facts are revealed.

It was late afternoon when a community member called Neighborhood Defender Service, where I worked at the time, to say Faith needed legal help. I was on intake with my colleague Laurie, so we immediately headed to the precinct where Faith was being questioned. Once there, we informed the captain that we were Faith's lawyers and demanded that all questioning stop immediately.

He was clearly surprised to see us, since people without private attorneys almost never have access to lawyers at this early, important stage of a criminal investigation. Grudgingly, he led us into the small room where Faith was seated. She was in her midthirties, and I could see that the experience was already taking a toll on her. She looked tired and was nervously playing with a tissue, looking around the room for any clues about what was going to happen next.

We introduced ourselves and calmly explained that we were there to defend her. She had never been in the criminal justice system before. As we explained the charges, it was clear that she was focused on one thing and one thing only—her children. "Where are they? Are they okay? When can I see them? What's going to happen to them?" she asked us frantically.

Faith's arrest had triggered not only a child welfare investigation into Jordan's injuries but also an inquiry regarding the safety of her two older children. By the time we got to Faith, the agency had already taken custody of her kids. Gently, we broke the news to her. Her face twisted with pain. Tears began streaming down her cheeks and onto her blouse. My heart tightened. I reached over the table and touched her hand.

"Ms. Stevens," I said, trying to maintain my composure, "I know this is hard. I promise you we will do everything we can to get your kids back and fight this case. It's going to take some time, but we will be there every step."

Sometimes the only thing you can do as a public defender is offer reassurance and help prepare your client psychologically for the battle ahead. You may not understand what the person is going through, but you know what a broken heart looks like, so you offer any comfort you can. In those moments, your law degree doesn't matter. Nothing you learned in law school is relevant. What counts is your willingness to see the other person without judgment and offer whatever support you can without expecting anything in return.

We knew that this was going to be a complex case, and we were preparing Faith for what was to come. She was going to face the power of government in two distinct ways. She would have to fight for her freedom and innocence in criminal court while simultaneously fighting for custody of her children in family court.

It would be years before I integrated legal strategies in the criminal and family systems at the Bronx Defenders, yet here I was, simply stunned by my own ignorance of this other world where something perhaps even more precious than liberty could be at stake—the bond with one's children.

Until I met Faith, I had never stepped foot in family court. As a public defender, it had never occurred to me that what happened in criminal court could impact a family court proceeding. Suddenly, I was filled with remorse and shame. I thought about all the parents I had defended in criminal court and how I had never even bothered to ask whether their arrest had triggered a child welfare investigation. I wondered how much harm my siloed approach to their criminal defense, and all those "good deals" I had worked so hard to negotiate for them, had inadvertently done to my clients and their families.

More shocking than my myopic public-defender worldview that only criminal cases mattered was the fact that I hadn't even realized that the government had the power to terminate a person's parental rights. Temporarily removing a child from a parent to protect them was one thing, but learning that the government could erase a parent's right to be a parent *forever* stunned me. It also became clear how this uniquely impacts women. According to census statistics, 80 percent of single-parent households in the U.S. are under the care of mothers, and nearly a third of these families live in poverty.[1]

No parent is perfect, but if you are a woman living in poverty, particularly a woman of color, the family court system will often view you through a harsher lens, holding you to a higher standard than wealthier parents. I had seen my fair share of mothers being dragged into family court, at risk of losing their parental rights for habitual marijuana use. But wealthy mothers who regularly downed Valium and gin and tonics when returning home from their corporate jobs never found themselves under the magnifying glass of the family court system.

Much the way police target people from low-income communities of color, the child welfare system focuses on those same communities. Crushing poverty easily becomes child neglect when you are Black or brown. Substance use becomes child abuse. I grew up with a father trapped in a cycle of drug addiction and a mother who wasn't always keeping tabs on where we were or what we were doing. I can tell you one thing: child protective services never came knocking on our door.

Although Faith's case was my first experience navigating the child welfare system, Laurie was a seasoned lawyer with years of experience in family court. I loved everything about her. Brilliant, funny, hardworking, and fiercely dedicated to her clients, Laurie taught me everything I needed to know about the strange new world of family court. With my experience as a public defender and hers in family court, we were a powerful duo prepared to fight for Faith in both systems.

Faith was indicted by a grand jury and faced seven counts of felony assault in criminal court—each count representing a bone that was broken.

A formal petition to remove Faith's children and terminate her parental rights was filed against her in family court. The battle lines were drawn. She was released without bail on the criminal case, this being her first and only involvement in the criminal justice system. Next, the child welfare system agreed to return Faith's two older children to her care after conducting extensive psychological examinations of both children, X-rays, and medical exams. Jordan, however, was placed with a new foster family.

The stakes couldn't have been higher for Faith and her children. If she was found guilty in the criminal case, she might go to prison. If she was found guilty in the family court case, she would never see Jordan again and might even lose custody of her biological children. Worse, she might have her parental rights terminated forever.

We received copies of the X-rays taken of Jordan's body and made appointments to see expert radiologists in some of New York City's best hospitals. We collected boxes and boxes of medical records detailing Jordan's entire history, starting with his birth. We hired a nurse to review every entry in the records so that we didn't miss a thing. We stayed up late into the night, poring over the notes from the child welfare interviews with Faith and her children. We spoke with Faith for hours, trying to understand how Jordan might have sustained the injuries. It was clear that she loved her children and tried to be a superb mother. It didn't seem possible that this diligent, dedicated woman could have harmed Jordan.

Getting help from medical experts turned out to be more challenging than I expected. Every time the X-rays were placed on the lit box for review by a doctor, we seemed to have stepped on the third rail. Doctor after doctor responded similarly: "This is classic child abuse. There are spiral fractures in both arms that happen when someone twists an arm with force, causing the bones to split in a spiral pattern. It's well established that these are the telltale signs of child abuse. I can't help you, Counselor." And with that, the conversation would end. They wanted nothing more to do with the case, or with us.

We were running out of options. At the time, I was pregnant with my first child. I don't know if it was the prospect of motherhood or just my single-mindedness when it came to client defense, but I refused to give up on Faith. A mother's pain is raw and palpable. I knew in my gut that there had to be a different explanation for how Jordan had been injured, and I promised Faith that we would leave no stone unturned.

And then we had our stroke of luck. Reviewing the baby's medical records for what must have been the hundredth time, we came across the name of another doctor who had examined Jordan at birth: Dr. Ibrahim. We looked him up. It just so happened that Dr. Ibrahim was also the head of the genetics department at one of the most prestigious hospitals in New York. My mind was racing. This had to be it.

We contacted Dr. Ibrahim and he invited us to his office. The morning of our meeting, we arrived early and sat in the reception area. When it was time, he emerged from his office with a warm smile and invited us in. Stacks of files and papers covered every inch of his desk. Books lined the small shelves, and his medical diplomas were prominently displayed on the wall. I noticed the X-rays that we had sent him attached to the small X-ray reader in his office. He welcomed us and asked if we wanted coffee.

"Dr. Ibrahim, thank you for seeing us," I began. "We saw that you were involved in Jordan's medical care when he was born and were hoping that you might give us some insights into his medical condition. As you know, his foster mother, our client, has criminal charges against her for the broken bones his pediatrician found at his last physical. We were hoping that you might shed some light on Jordan's medical condition so that we have better context for the injuries."

Without missing a beat, Dr. Ibrahim solved the puzzle the others had ignored.

"I was in the delivery room when this young child was born," he replied. "I indicated then that his underlying genetic disorder, arthrogryposis multiplex congenita, would mean that his bones would be very susceptible to breaks and fractures. The condition means that there is insufficient muscle mass surrounding the bones, which in a normal child would protect them from harm to their bones."

He turned on the backlight so we could see the X-rays. "See these bone fractures? Do you notice anything about them?"

I answered that we had been informed by several doctors that they were spiral fractures.

"Yes," he said, "some of them are, but there is something else. If you look at the pattern of breaks, including the spiral fractures, you can see that they are completely symmetrical. There are breaks in the same places but on different arms and legs. Except for one break—the left femur bone—the other six are symmetrical. If this were child abuse, you would expect to see random injuries in different locations. Here you see the same location but on different limbs."

Bingo.

"In my opinion," Dr. Ibrahim went on, "these fractures were caused by the repeated range-of-motion exercises that were part of his physical therapy regimens at the agency and at home, not by child abuse. The foster mom was doing what she was told to do by the physical therapists, but she was breaking his bones over and over again without knowing it."

We asked Dr. Ibrahim if he would be willing to testify as an expert on Faith's case and he agreed. Now we had a fighting chance.

The following week, we arrived in family court for the trial that would decide whether Faith's parental rights would be terminated. There are no juries in family court proceedings in New York City, so we had to convince a judge of Faith's innocence. Usually that's almost an impossible task, because most judges reflexively side with government and prosecutors. But here we were fortunate enough to be in front of an experienced, smart judge willing to listen to all the evidence before jumping to conclusions.

During opening statements to the court, corporation counsel, an attorney assigned to represent Jordan in this proceeding, was predictably strident about their belief that child abuse had caused the injuries to Jordan. Their star witness was the pediatrician who had discovered the fractures and reported Faith.

Dr. Larsen was tall, Nordic-looking, and elegantly dressed. His self-confidence was obvious as he took the witness stand. He gave a full accounting of his educational background and good deeds as a doctor, including that he had dedicated much of his life to treating babies who were HIV positive. He talked about discovering Jordan's broken bones during a routine pediatric visit and about his fervent belief that only child abuse could have caused them.

As I watched him, I wondered if he ever thought it was strange that the same woman he believed had viciously broken seven bones in Jordan's body could be the same woman who had religiously brought Jordan in for regular visits knowing that he was going to have a full physical exam. The notes from the visits with Dr. Larsen were rife with references to the thoughtful questions Faith asked, the care she exhibited toward Jordan, and her diligence about regularly exercising his limbs as directed by the physical therapists. So how did he go from being the doctor who admired her vigilance and caregiving to the man on the stand trying to terminate her parental rights? What led him to instantly assume that Faith had abused Jordan rather than seek other medical opinions or explore alternative explanations?

Certainly it wasn't lack of intelligence. I could not help but wonder what his reaction might have been if the foster mother had been an affluent white parent from a community closer to his own. Would he have given her the benefit of the doubt? I couldn't prove it, but I knew in my bones that this was about race and class. Fortunately, we had Dr. Ibrahim on our side to counter Dr. Larsen's assumptions.

Dr. Larsen finished his testimony by reiterating that the injuries could not be from anything other than child abuse. His unfounded certainty was beginning to get under my skin.

It was now Dr. Ibrahim's turn to take the stand. In many ways, he was the opposite of Dr. Larsen. Black, soft-spoken, and with a slight accent from his Nigerian roots, he had none of Dr. Larsen's swagger. His suit wasn't elegant, his shoes were slightly scuffed, and he paused to think about each of his answers before speaking.

For the next hour, he answered my questions with precision, thoughtfulness, and candor. He walked us through Jordan's birth, diagnosis, and various medical conditions until he got to the recent X-rays.

"Dr. Ibrahim, have you had a chance to review Jordan's X-rays from his physical exam with Dr. Larsen?" I asked.

"I have," he answered.

"And what are your conclusions about how those injuries were sustained?"

I knew what was coming, but my heart was still pounding.

"Given the symmetrical nature of the fractures, those injuries were not the result of Jordan being hit or abused by anyone. They were caused by the physical therapy exercises that were prescribed for him. Each time someone rotated his limbs or put him in a crawling position, he could have sustained those breaks. They wouldn't cause injuries in a normal child, but his bones are too vulnerable for them. Anyone who conducted those exercises could have caused those injuries without ever knowing it."

With all the evidence in, it was time for the judge to issue her decision. She ruled in Faith's favor, accepting every bit of Dr. Ibrahim's testimony. We were elated, and nothing could take that away, even when the judge felt compelled to express her great respect and admiration for Dr. Larsen and his "valiant" efforts to save babies with HIV. There are times when you just need to keep your mouth shut and take the win. This was one of them. Besides, the battle wasn't over—Faith's criminal case remained.

In civil cases, as in family court, government officials must prove their case by a preponderance of the evidence. In criminal court, the burden of proof is higher because one's physical liberty is at stake. That means a criminal case must be proved beyond a reasonable doubt. Of course, the legal standards of proof were completely irrelevant to Faith. She would have gone to jail over and over if it meant that she could ultimately regain custody of Jordan and her children.

With the family court case behind us, we began to focus on the criminal case. The government had failed to prove the case in family court, where there is a lower burden of proof, so how would it be able to prove its case beyond a reasonable doubt?

Clearly, Dr. Ibrahim's medical opinion in and of itself created that doubt. Even better, we would get to present our defense to a jury of twelve New Yorkers—almost always better than putting the decision in the hands of a judge.

But our confidence didn't allow us to relax. We both knew that trials were unpredictable, and ours was going to be in the courtroom of a senior judge whose imperious style was only slightly more obnoxious than her penchant for department store shopping during work hours.

The prosecutor assigned to the case was notoriously strident.

Like most prosecutors, once she landed on a target for prosecution to demonize, it was almost impossible for facts to break through. We would have to depend on the jury for that.

We appeared in court ready for jury selection on a Monday morning in early fall. It was my favorite time of year in New York. The hot, humid summer was finally replaced by crisp fall nights, trees turning remarkable colors, and, for me, the Jewish holidays of Rosh Hashanah and Yom Kippur.

While I am not particularly religious, I love these High Holy Days of reflection, renewal, and contemplation. It is an opportunity to reflect on the past year, apologize to those you've hurt, forgive, vow to do better, and welcome a new year with a full heart. It turned out that Faith's trial was beginning the week of Yom Kippur—the highest holy day of the year, which would require me to attend services in synagogue and fast for twenty-four hours. Naively, we assumed that the presiding judge would simply honor the holiday for the necessary twenty-four hours, so we started the selection process.

The first couple of days were unremarkable. Predictably, many people asked to be excused once they heard that Faith was charged with seven counts of felony assault against a toddler. The jurors who remained seemed thoughtful, albeit predominantly white and affluent and living a world away from Faith. We held on to the fact that Manhattan juries are liberal by most standards, even though when it comes to crime, especially crime involving minors, the most progressive people can't be trusted to suspend biases and focus purely on the evidence. We knew we could not take anything for granted.

As the week drew to an end, we still hadn't completed jury selection. Yom Kippur was a day away. "Judge," I explained, "in order to honor the holiday, my cocounsel and I must be home tomorrow several hours before sundown so that we can eat and travel to synagogue before Yom Kippur begins. If we end tomorrow by two p.m., we will be fine. I just wanted to mention it now so that we can schedule today and tomorrow appropriately."

The judge looked down at me over her reading glasses and replied, "I will take your application into consideration, Counselor. Let's proceed and see what happens."

Certain that I must have misunderstood her meaning, I sought clarification. "We are happy to proceed, but you will allow us to leave tomorrow by two p.m., right?"

She stared right at me. "Counselor, I said that I would consider the application. Let's see what happens tomorrow."

I looked at Laurie, whose mouth was agape. "Is she kidding?" she whispered to me. I reassured her that it would be fine, even though I knew that if the judge wouldn't adjourn on time tomorrow, we would be forced to choose between walking out of the courtroom at 2:00 p.m., risking being held in contempt by her, and continuing the jury-selection process, risking not being able to follow our holiday's prescription.

I looked up at the judge. I could see that she was enjoying our discomfort. "Fine, Judge, we will see what happens tomorrow,"

I said, holding fast to my belief that when it comes to judges, it is better to never let them see your vulnerability.

She waited until noon the next day to let us know that she would adjourn the case for the holiday—a strange exercise of power that presaged the tenor of the upcoming trial.

Opening statements are not supposed to be argument—that is reserved for the end of the trial—but most prosecutors can't resist letting the demonizing of the accused begin. Our prosecutor was no exception. Her opening statement was rife with emotion and accusation. We sat stone-faced, scribbling nothing of importance on a yellow legal pad to keep ourselves calm. Finally she sat down, and it was our turn.

Although defense counsel does not have to give an opening statement, I have never passed up the opportunity to speak to the jury. Many defense lawyers do not give opening statements, arguing that they don't have the burden to prove anything, so they would rather not disclose their defense. Perhaps that would make sense if, in fact, the burden of proof was genuinely carried only by the prosecution in a criminal case. But the reality is that before the evidentiary part of a trial even begins, most jurors have already formed an opinion of the accused. It is difficult to change impressions once they are made. Most people think if you've been arrested, there must have been "a good reason for it." To think otherwise requires you to accept that sometimes people make false allegations against others, or that police arrests are not always legal.

For people who have never been targeted by law enforcement

or who live outside those communities that are, the idea that innocent people are rounded up by the police with some regularity seems conspiratorial. Similarly, the idea that a prosecutor would overcharge a person with crimes they know they can't prove at trial but that will intimidate the defendant into pleading guilty to a lesser offense during plea bargaining appears far-fetched. Mindful of this, I never missed the opportunity to provide an opening statement, not only to humanize the person I represented but also to prime the jury to ask critical questions and withhold quick judgments.

I began my opening statement describing Faith as the loving mother that she was, preparing the jury for Dr. Ibrahim's testimony, and questioning the validity of Dr. Larsen's medical opinion about the cause of the injuries. The prosecutor could barely sit in her seat, interrupting us at every turn with frivolous objections. The judge ruled in her favor almost every time. If we had any doubts about where the judge's allegiance lay, they were quickly extinguished. We were fighting both the prosecution and the judge.

As the case went on, the judge's disdain became more obvious. The expression of disgust on her face and her frequent eye rolling must have been noticeable to the jury. I hoped that the jury could see the bias and rebalance the power dynamic in the courtroom. Juries can do incredible things. Once I saw a jury return a verdict of not guilty, explaining to the judge they were so appalled by the incompetence of the defense counsel that they ignored what happened during the trial. Instead, they reenacted the case in the jury room and reached the verdict they believed would have happened if the accused had had competent counsel. It was a stunning rebuke of the system and a spectacular display of the jury's commitment to fairness. It doesn't happen often, but when it does, it's magical.

Finally, it was time for a repeat of the battle of experts we had fought in family court. Dr. Larsen was in his element in Manhattan Supreme Court. As he entered the huge, cavernous courtroom, all eyes were on him. He seemed to love the attention. The prosecutor qualified him as a pediatric expert by asking him to recount his medical training and experience. Again he focused on his work with HIV-positive babies, and you could feel the jury's admiration.

I wasn't worried. After all, Dr. Ibrahim had been in the delivery room when Jordan was born and had more knowledge about his underlying medical condition. More significantly, he wasn't just a pediatrician. He was the head of an entire genetics department and an expert in the specific disease that rendered Jordan's bones vulnerable to injury. In the end, it all boiled down to whose medical opinion the jury would believe.

Dr. Ibrahim's testimony was clear, clinical, and unwavering. The jury listened intently.

Once the evidentiary part of the trial was over, the judge adjourned the case until the following morning for closing statements. I knew it was going to be a long night, but I was excited about the chance to sum up the evidence for the jury and argue for Faith's innocence.

Lawyers have all sorts of superstitions they follow during trial, especially as summation approaches. Some have specific clothes they wear on the day of summation, from lucky ties to a certain color. We create unshakable rituals, lest we tempt the verdict Fates. I was no exception. That night, as I laid out my long legal pads and the blue felt-tip markers that I used to pen every summation I have ever given, I began to write—in longhand—every word that I wanted to say to the jury. We are trained as young lawyers to not rely on notes, but that requires both a kind of self-confidence and a memory that I simply never had. I write out everything ahead of time, in excruciating detail, even if I never read a word of it.

Starting strong and ending strong are critical in persuasive argument, so I thought seriously about how I wanted to begin this summation. It was clear to me that race and poverty had made Faith a convenient scapegoat for the failures of the child welfare system and the medical profession to properly understand and protect Jordan. The criminal justice system was all too complicit in absolving them of any responsibility and directing all the ire at Faith.

Facts are the foundation of a good defense, but only stories can make them come alive. Stories are the pathway into people's psychology, and here I needed to undo some hardwired biases and tap into the jurors' sense of injustice. I decided to start my opening statement with a Bible story, the story of Leviticus.

In Leviticus, members of a community gather their sins and load them on the back of a goat. They then send the goat out into the desert, hoping to alleviate themselves of the burden and guilt of their failures. It was a perfect parable for this situation that would allow me to capture the jurors' imaginations. I would begin with it and build my case from there.

The next morning, the courtroom was filled with people. Many of my colleagues were there to support us, and the prosecutor had her own fan club in the audience. The defense goes first, a disadvantage but one that can be overcome by anticipating what the prosecutor is going to say and countering it. I stood up to deliver my summation and walked over to the podium in front of the jury. Looking into the eyes of the jurors, glancing back to look at Faith only when I referred to her, I began my summation.

The prosecutor objected frequently, and I could see that the judge was becoming increasingly angry at me—not because I was doing anything wrong but because, judging by the jurors' faces, I was being effective. As expected, she allowed the prosecutor's interruptions, often admonishing me to "move on." At the end of the summation, I walked over to the defense table, positioned myself so that the jurors had to look at Faith, and asked them to find her not guilty of all seven counts. Next it was the prosecutor's turn. Predictably, she rested her entire case on Dr. Larsen's testimony.

The case went to the jury, and now we had to wait. Jurors frequently have questions for the judge during their deliberations. Sometimes they want testimony read to them; other times they just want some direction from the court. This jury was no exception.

After several hours of deliberations, a note came out from the jury. I saw the court officer hand the note to the judge. She read it and then announced, "Officer, bring the jurors in, please." I was confused. The law is clear that both defense counsel and the prosecutor are entitled to see the jury note and argue to the court what they think the response should be to the jury's inquiry.

Knowing that I had to arm myself with every possible recourse for a potential appeal, I stood up right away. "Judge, we haven't had a chance to see the jury note, so why are you calling in the jury?"

The judge barely looked at me. "Officer, bring in the jury. Counselor, sit down."

I persisted. "Judge, we are entitled to see the jury note and be heard before you call them back in here and respond to their note."

"Sit down, Counselor. I will decide what you do and don't get to see. Now, sit down right now. I've heard enough from you."

I stood my ground. "Judge, I just want to make clear for the record that this is a critical stage of the proceeding, and you are denying my client effective representation, indeed *any* representation, at this critical moment by denying us the ability to see the jury note and make argument about how the court should respond."

She didn't even bother to reply. Instead, the court officer led the jurors back into the courtroom, where they took their original seats. The judge proceeded to answer some of their questions relating to the medical testimony and instructed the court clerk to read back portions of the testimony.

Sometimes you play the long game as a trial lawyer. The truth was that the specific content of the jury note that the judge had so vehemently hidden from me was largely inconsequential to the trial, but her actions were not. She was making an error of constitutional magnitude, and I knew it. Her hatred of me had driven her to refuse to engage with me at all, leaving a conviction—if there was going to be one—open to the possibility of a successful appeal.

Even though appeals are almost never won by the defense, here the error was significant. Of course, the prosecutor could have protected the record by asking the judge to show us the note, but in her zeal to win, she chose to sit back and be complicit in the judge's denial of a fundamental right.

We were at a local diner with Faith when we got word that the jury had reached a verdict. We gathered our belongings, paid our check, and made our way back to the courthouse. Faith asked what I thought was going to happen and I answered truthfully: we had done everything we could do, and I felt good about our chances of winning. What I didn't share was that I felt like throwing up, a feeling I have every time a verdict is about to come in. It is the most terrifying moment in the trial. Everything is on the line, there is nothing else you can do at that point, and you are completely at the mercy of twelve strangers.

Faith was scared but ready. "Will the defendant please rise," said the judge, peering at the verdict sheet. We all stood up together—Faith, Laurie, and me. The judge flinched and asked us—the lawyers—to sit down.

I have never understood how defense lawyers can sit when a verdict is being read, leaving their client alone at this crucial and life-changing moment. "Judge, we prefer to stand with our client, but thank you," I said.

She rolled her eyes and turned her head to the jury. "Will the foreperson please read the verdict."

Faith reached for my arm, and I took her hand in mine, squeezing it as the jury foreperson rose.

The judge began: "On count one of the indictment, assault in the second degree, how does the jury find the defendant?"

"Not guilty," the foreperson responded.

"On count two of the indictment, assault in the second degree, how does the jury find the defendant?"

"Not guilty."

"On count three of the indictment, assault in the second degree, how does the jury find the defendant?"

"Not guilty."

We were almost halfway through the seven counts of the indictment, and I could feel Faith relaxing. Standing on the other side of Faith, Laurie started to smile. I continued to squeeze Faith's hand.

"On count four of the indictment, assault in the second degree, how does the jury find the defendant?"

"Not guilty."

"On count five of the indictment, assault in the second degree, how does the jury find the defendant?"

"Not guilty."

"On count six of the indictment, assault in the second degree, how does the jury find the defendant?"

"Not guilty."

We were almost there.

"And on count seven of the indictment, assault in the second degree, how does the jury find the defendant?"

"Guilty."

For a moment, I thought I had misheard what the foreperson said. Faith turned to me, panic in her eyes. Laurie looked over at me, shaking her head, as she grabbed Faith's other hand. We stood there, three women holding hands, unable to move or speak.

The judge quickly thanked the jury for their service and excused them from the courtroom. Then, without missing a beat, she announced: "The defendant is remanded without bail to the custody of the Department of Corrections."

Still reeling from the verdict, I quickly snapped back into fight mode. "Judge, there is absolutely no justification for remanding Ms. Stevens into jail. She has made every single court appearance for over two years. She has no prior criminal record, and she has two children at home waiting for her this evening. She was acquitted of six of the seven counts and she is probation eligible. There is no question but that she will come back to court for sentencing. There is absolutely no reason to put this woman in jail and send her to Rikers Island today, and to do so would cause irreparable harm not only to her but to her two children as well. Please, Judge, I would ask that you allow her to remain out of custody until sentencing."

But the judge had all the power, and she knew it.

"Officers, take the defendant into custody. Sentencing will be in one month. See you all then." With that, and a self-satisfied smile, she stood up and left the courtroom.

Faith was speechless. The court officers came with handcuffs. I motioned them to give us a minute. With Laurie standing by my side, I put my arms around Faith and whispered in her ear: "You can do this. It's scary but you can do it. We will make sure the kids are okay. We will come see you this week, and we will do everything in our power to get you out, Faith. I promise. The court officers are going to take you into custody. It will be a hard night, but you can do this. I have to let you go now, Faith. I don't want to, but I have to."

I loosened my hug and stepped back. Tears were dripping down my face and the court officers could barely look my way. "Thank you," I whispered to them as they closed in on Faith, shackling her as we watched helplessly. Then they led her away, leaving Laurie and me in the courtroom alone.

"What the f—k?" said Laurie, breaking her silence. "How could they have done that? They acquit her on six bone breaks but convict her on the seventh? How does that make any sense?"

Pulling myself together, I tried to make sense of it. "It was a compromise. Someone wanted to convict her, and this was how they found consensus," I responded, still struggling.

As we got ready to leave the courtroom and head uptown, I realized that we had no idea which bone the jury had convicted Faith of breaking. Before the trial began, we had asked the judge to require the prosecutor to either consolidate all the counts into one or require them to delineate which count referred to which broken bone, but she had denied my motion outright. During the trial this had been like fighting with a hand tied behind our back, but now Her Honor's cruelty could give us a new card to play if we won the appeal and the case was returned for a retrial. This battle was far from over.

For now, we had to focus on how to get Faith out of Rikers Island. Fortunately, her kids were able to stay with her sister while we waited for sentencing day, giving her some peace of mind as she endured what would be weeks of confinement.

On the day of sentencing, we arrived in court with an arsenal of reasons why probation was the only justifiable sentence. She had already served over a month in jail, which we hoped would satisfy the judge's lust for retribution.

We presented a twenty-page sentencing memo, messages from Faith's children, and a host of other letters of support. We knew that Faith was facing a maximum sentence of two and a third to seven years in state prison, the harshest sentence allowed for a second-degree assault conviction, but we thought there was a chance that the judge would sentence her to what was called a "split sentence," one where she would serve six months in jail and the remaining four and a half years on probation.

The judge was no happier to see us on sentencing day than she had been during the course of the trial. She barely listened to our sentencing argument. It was clear she had already made up her mind. "Will the defendant please rise," she intoned. We all stood up, and like a punch to the stomach, she delivered her decision: "The defendant is hereby sentenced to two and a third to seven years in state prison. Counselor, advise her of her rights to appeal."

It was time to put our next strategy into motion. I had already ordered the transcript of the trial, including the back-and-forth over whether I would be allowed to see the jury notes. We were going to head to the Appellate Division—the court between the trial court and the Court of Appeals—which had the power to grant a "stay of execution of sentence," holding the sentence off until the appellate issues could be heard and resolved. We had researched which judges were in the Appellate Division on which dates and made sure to have our motion heard before Judge Jimenez, the only Latino judge on the appellate court at the time and the only one I thought would give us a fair shot.

Walking into his chambers several days later, we were warmly greeted by Judge Jimenez. Our motion to stay the sentence, along with the minutes we had attached to the motion, was on his desk. He smiled at us and then looked over at the appellate prosecutor, who was new to the case.

"Counselor," Judge Jimenez said, "if it is true that the court refused to allow defense counsel to even see the jury notes, much less comment on them, how do you expect to defend this conviction and win at the appellate level when the conviction itself is challenged?"

The prosecutor shrugged his shoulders, faintly smiling, and said simply, "We can't, Your Honor." And with that, the stay of execution of sentence was granted, and Faith was released from jail pending the appeal.

Eventually we won the appeal, and the conviction was reversed over the jury-note fiasco. Faith remained free and the case was sent back to the trial court for a retrial. Since there were six counts of the indictment on which Faith was already acquitted, the prosecution could go forward only on the one remaining count, count seven. It was time to use our second card.

We were now in front of a new judge, who read our motion to dismiss the case entirely with great interest. Since we didn't know which bones Faith had been acquitted of breaking and which she was convicted of, it would be impossible to retry her without violating the double jeopardy clause of the Fifth Amendment—the prohibition against trying someone for something that they have already been found not guilty of. The new judge saw the problem and dismissed the case outright.

It was finally over. Faith picked up her life as best she could and returned to parenting her two biological children. But she never got to see baby Jordan again.

Over the years, I would represent many women like Faith, women whose eyes would always take me back to those days in the Bedford Hills prison when I promised myself to never look away from injustice—to never forget those relegated to the oblivion and darkness of prisons and jails. Faith endured two years of pain and humiliation, the hell of Rikers Island, losing baby Jordan, and the possibility of losing her own children. But still she rose, time and time again, to fight back.

It was from women like Faith that I learned courage, and it was for women like Faith that, twenty-five years later, I would find myself moving halfway across the country to Oklahoma, ground zero of women's mass incarceration in America, to once again reimagine public defense.

8

Comfort Zone versus Uncomfortable Truths

The jail administrator led the way. It was a long, white hall and our steps echoed loudly as we made our way to one of the "women's pods." We arrived at a huge metal door and a young guard, no older than my own son, buzzed us in. Inside, a large, cavernous space spread over two levels, each lined with scores of identical jail cells. The guard's desk was centrally located, panopticon style, offering a full view of every cell and the women in orange jumpsuits walking around. One by one, their eyes turned toward me with curiosity. There were women of many races—Black, Native American, Latina, white— some barely of age.

Standing in the center of the space, his arms crossed over his belly, the jail administrator remarked that this pod, like all the other women's pods, was completely full. "You know," he said, "we incarcerate a lot of women here in Oklahoma."

The year was 2016. Hillary Clinton was running for president. Justice Sonia Sotomayor, the third woman appointed to the Supreme Court, had joined us at the Bronx Defenders for a big public event. And I was beginning to plan a leadership transition in my office to an executive team composed of women. As an avid feminist, I considered this a good year—at least to this point— and a far cry from when I had started my career trading sharp elbows in rooms full of men.

And yet here I was, standing in the middle of a jail filled to the brim with other women. In the intervening decades, the number of incarcerated women and girls in the United States had increased by more than 700 percent, growing twice as fast as the incarceration rate for men.[1]

Oklahoma had, by far, the highest rate of female incarceration.[2] While women were making progress in a variety of fields, incarceration, in my opinion, has always been the true indicator of where society is heading. The fact that women are the fastest-growing incarcerated population in America is no coincidence.

I had come to Tulsa, Oklahoma, at the invitation of Amy Santee from the George Kaiser Family Foundation, to help train the local public defender office on the Bronx Defenders model of holistic defense. We had already done this type of training in other jurisdictions through a grant from the U.S. Department of Justice, which had taken me everywhere from Boston to Texas to Alaska to the Flathead Indian Reservation in Montana. The jail visit was part of the itinerary Amy and her team had arranged to give me the lay of the land.

Little did I know, I would fall hard for Oklahoma.

I still remember the first day I stepped foot in Tulsa. As my evening flight descended into the Tulsa International Airport, the pilot came on the loudspeaker: "Good evening, folks. We are about to start our descent into Tulsa. The current temperature is ninety-four degrees, with light winds out of the south. It should be a smooth landing, so buckle up, and thank you for traveling with us tonight. We will have you on the ground shortly."

I looked at the stranger next to me. "It's eleven o'clock at night. Did he just say it's ninety-four degrees?" I asked, thinking I must have misheard him. Looking at me with a faint, amused smile, she responded: "Yes, he did. Honey, it's Oklahoma." That was the first of many lessons I would eventually have to learn about what it means to be Oklahoma.

Over the next six months, I visited Tulsa many times, trying to learn everything I could about its criminal justice system. I went to court with the public defenders, watched trials and court proceedings, spent time at the local jail, and made note of the demographics and zip codes where most of the people cycling through the jail came from. I spoke with judges, social service providers, and local lawyers.

The more I learned, the more troubled I became. The culture of the criminal courthouse in Tulsa was one steeped in the belief that all the players in the system—public defenders and prosecutors alike—were on the same team. There wasn't a strong, adversarial public defense system—critical to the protection of due process—and creating one would be particularly hard.

Tulsa's legal community was small and operated like a provincial small town. Judges and prosecutors, defenders, and members of the private bar frequented the same restaurants, sent their kids to the same schools, and coached soccer teams together on the weekends. Getting along was paramount.

I had been a public defender long enough to know that the people who suffer from that kind of courthouse familiarity are the people most on the outside—the poor and marginalized, whose cases make up the largest share of the courts' dockets.

Back in New York City, there were some good lawyers I knew who established personal relationships with prosecutors and judges, but I wasn't one of them. I never wanted to walk into a courtroom and have the person I was tasked with representing see me cozying up to the people prosecuting or incarcerating them. I didn't want to feel compromised when I fought hard on behalf of a client. I had seen the dangers of what happens when people close ranks, and I didn't want to risk being a part of that. I never wanted to feel personally indebted to the other side for their friendship, kindness, or even payment for a round of drinks at a bar after a long day at work. But mostly I stayed away from them because of their willing participation in a system that, while theoretically well designed, was all too often rendered indefensible in practice. It was a disqualifier that I just couldn't get over.

It was easy to maintain my distance in a place as big as New York City, but Tulsa was a small pond and would challenge the viability of my line-in-the-sand approach.

Perhaps more troubling than the courthouse culture and women's incarceration rates was what I learned about the city itself. I noticed a railroad track running through town. I would watch the trains go through, marveling at the long line of boxcars and romanticizing the sound of the train whistle late at night.

At first I didn't notice that, during my visits, my time was spent mostly on only one side of those train tracks, the south side, where the courthouse and public defender offices were located, along with most restaurants and hotels. The jail was located right on the dividing line between north and south. It wasn't until my third trip to Tulsa that I began to hear whispers about the horrifying history that lay next to those beautiful old railroad tracks.

The Tulsa race massacre of 1921 was one of the worst instances of racial terror and murder in American history. Hundreds were injured. Thousands were displaced. What ignited the massacre is not in dispute. A young Black man was in an elevator with a white woman and inadvertently bumped into her, an occurrence that, but for racialized fear and hatred, would have gone unnoticed.

A rumor spread that she had been sexually assaulted—the racist trope trotted out in America to justify arresting, imprisoning, or even murdering Black men. In Tulsa, this incident unleashed what had always been there just beneath the surface: an intense racial hatred and jealousy of the Black community of Green-wood, then one of the most affluent and successful Black com-munities in America.

A mob descended on the jail where the young man was held. Fearing that he would be lynched like others before him, com-munity members from Greenwood came to his defense. Tensions escalated and all hell broke loose. It took only two days for white mobs to burn to the ground what Black Tulsans had built over generations. What white mobs couldn't finish, local law enforce-ment did when they dropped turpentine bombs on the commu-nity, reducing Black-owned businesses, homes, and churches to ashes.

After learning this history, I began to spend more and more time in north Tulsa, where many people from the local Black community still lives to this day. There was beauty, family, and faith but also the scars of marginalization, racism, and poverty, which could be seen everywhere. It was very different from the Bronx yet also familiar. It had a similar spirit of resilience, but the communities were also similar in the mirror they held to the rest of society, revealing our complicity in maintaining the sta-tus quo.

When Amy finally sat me down and asked how ready I thought the Tulsa County Public Defender's Office was to incor-porate the principles of holistic defense, I knew the answer. It would be like Sisyphus pushing the boulder up the hill.

Gently I explained that the office and the culture of the local criminal justice system had a very long way to go. What I didn't

tell her then was that many Tulsa public defenders barely interviewed their clients before their first court appearance, much less
displayed much interest in deepening and expanding their advocacy
services. As far as I could tell, not a single public defender I spoke
with had ever visited a client on the north side or had much of an
understanding of or appreciation for the historical context of their
clients' community. I was willing to provide training but wasn't
optimistic that the local office would embrace the approach.

Unfazed, Amy said, "I have an idea. Stay with me, now. What
if we started something entirely new here in Tulsa? Do you think
we could build an office here and model it after the Bronx Defenders?" I was intrigued.

She went on, "And what if the office, which our foundation
would fund, only represented mothers who were arrested? I mean,
it fits into the foundation's focus, and since Oklahoma incarcerates
more women than anyone else, it would make so much sense.
Would you be willing to start that here? Is that crazy?"

Of course it was crazy. I was already running the Bronx Defenders, by then a 350-person organization. We had been through
hell and back during the "Hands Up" controversy and were just
beginning to regain our footing.

I had always dreamed that the Bronx Defenders would influence other public defender offices to transform from traditional
defenders to more holistic, client-centered ones, but I had never
contemplated starting another public defender office as an actual
project of the Bronx Defenders. And I had certainly never thought
about doing so in the buckle of the Bible Belt. Starting something

new, as an outsider coming into a closed legal system, would be challenging. Balancing my time between Oklahoma and the Bronx would be complicated, and convincing people from my office to move to Oklahoma to start this office with me would be nearly impossible. It was an impractical and outlandish idea. I had to say yes.

I had only one requirement—that we build the office in north Tulsa and prioritize serving the women in that community. I have always believed that one should go where the need is greatest and the history most egregious. Clearly, that was north Tulsa, and Amy agreed.

I returned to New York and announced that I was going to start a holistic defender office in Tulsa, Oklahoma, for women with children. My executive team looked at me like I had two heads, but they also knew me well enough to accept the fact that once I set my sights on an idea, I would make it a reality one way or another.

For the next six months I traveled to and from Oklahoma, mapping out how to create and launch the office. I identified space for the new office and spoke with stakeholders. With the cooperation of the jail administration, I conducted focus groups at the jail to better understand the experiences and needs of the women who were incarcerated.

These sessions were inspiring and heartbreaking. Huddled together in a circle, often linking arms as they spoke, woman after woman shared her story and experiences within the criminal justice system. When we asked how many of them had been victims of sexual violence, most, if not all, hands went up. Substance use and depression were the norm. There was an overwhelming distrust of their public defenders, and they had virtually no faith that anything in the system would change or that anyone cared. Without exception, the mothers in the group focused more on what was going to happen to their children than on what lay ahead for them. Surprisingly, they all seemed to know that Oklahoma incarcerated more women than anywhere else in the country. When I asked why they thought that was the case, the answer was almost always the same: "They just hate women down here."

It was hard to disagree. Sitting in court watching routine proceedings against women, my blood boiled with anger. It wasn't just the misuse of the court system to punish people who needed drug treatment, counseling, or simply a living wage and a safe place to live. It was the sheer cruelty with which prosecutors and judges decided women's fates, specifically mothers', once they were deemed unredeemable or unworthy of their children. It was clear that as a mother you were placed on a pedestal so others knew where to aim their stones.

The impact extended far beyond each individual woman in the system.

Eighty percent of women in jails are mothers, as are more than half the women serving sentences in state prisons.[3] Notably, the majority of women in our prisons and jails are charged with nonviolent offenses.[4] Unlike incarcerated men who are fathers, most incarcerated mothers were also the primary providers for their children prior to incarceration.[5] Incarceration sends their children to live with relatives or into foster care. States can move to terminate a person's parental rights when the child has been in the foster care system for fifteen of the last twenty-two months, and most mothers in prison are serving sentences longer than two years.[6]

Studies have found that children who are in foster care are several times more likely to experience sexual violence than children who stay with their biological parents.[7] According to data from the Bureau of Justice Statistics, about 10 percent of women in state prisons were in the foster care system themselves.[8] It's a vicious cycle of intergenerational trauma fueled by our society's overreliance on carceral responses.

The urgency of combining criminal defense and free representation for women in child-removal and parental-termination proceedings could not have been more obvious. Our track record of doing so at the Bronx Defenders positioned us well to adapt this strategy to the situation of mothers incarcerated in Oklahoma.

And so, in September 2016, I packed up my old Volvo station wagon; put my aging dog, Magic, in the back; picked up my best friend, Mitchell, who had agreed to accompany me on the drive from New York to Oklahoma; and headed to the buckle of the Bible Belt.

I was excited, particularly because a small but talented group of lawyers and advocates from the Bronx Defenders had decided to join me in the effort to build what would become the country's first public defender office designed to represent only women with children in the criminal justice system.

We decided to call the office Still She Rises, a tribute to Dr. Maya Angelou, who brilliantly described Black women's resiliency in the face of overt oppression and misogyny in her poem "And Still I Rise." It was one of my proudest moments, marrying my two loves—public defense and feminism—and taking what we had built in the South Bronx to serve the women of north Tulsa.

Starting up any new organization is always a whirlwind. I learned that as part of the original team at Neighborhood Defender Service in Harlem, and when I started the Bronx Defenders. I knew that it meant working long hours, having complex conversations, listening to heartfelt opinions, building a team culture, and leaning into the inevitable rifts that develop, both personally and organizationally, when things move from vision to reality. Leadership requires hearing everyone out but also knowing what is up for negotiation and what is not and being honest about that with your team. Over time, the parameters can shift, but what you are building, how, for whom, and why must be centered in every conversation.

Life in Tulsa was everything I expected and more. We opened our office in a virtually abandoned strip mall, and I ended up settling in an old house with a big porch and a massive oak tree.

My closest neighbors were a young couple and their pet pig, Kevin Bacon. With my friend Mitchell, I toured every secondhand shop and antique store within a five-mile radius and slowly put together my new home. One afternoon, I was walking downtown when a tornado siren started blaring. Seeing my expression, a local resident instructed me to go home, grab myself a cocktail, and settle in for the show as dark, ominous clouds gathered in the horizon. As my seatmate on the plane had said during that first flight to Tulsa: "Honey, it's Oklahoma."

I will be forever grateful to that small but mighty team who left their lives in New York to start Still She Rises with me. One of the first people to join me in Tulsa was Ruth, a young criminal defense lawyer from the Bronx Defenders.

Ruth had rented a studio in Owen Park, up the hill from my home, and I was helping her set it up. I adored Ruth. She was simultaneously a ferocious advocate and a gentle soul, and there was nothing she wouldn't do for a client lucky enough to have her as their lawyer.

One afternoon she asked if I would accompany her to Home Depot to see if we could find materials for a kitchen counter. We wandered up and down the expansive aisles until we found a large metal workbench that could double as a counter. It was incredibly heavy, and one of the Home Depot workers helped load it onto a hand truck for us. We pushed it up toward the shortest checkout line we could find. Behind us was a tall white man waiting his turn. He was holding twelve-by-twelve-inch kitchen tiles in his hands.

"Excuse me," he said. "Do you ladies want some help getting that home?" Ruth looked surprised, but I had been in Tulsa long enough to know that people will chat with you about anything, anywhere. It was an entirely different way of being for me, but one that I was growing to really appreciate. I told him that we were fine and thanked him for his concern. "Okay," he said, "but my mother is outside waiting for me in our pickup truck, and we can drive that for you." Ruth looked more and more concerned.

"That's so nice of you," I said. "Where are you and your mother driving? I wouldn't want you to go out of your way."

"It's all right, we're heading north. We just came down for these tiles. We can meet you outside."

He seemed to be around thirty and was wearing jeans and a plaid shirt. There was absolutely no edge to him, just sincerity. Realizing that there was no chance we would be able to fit the workbench into Ruth's small car, I accepted his invitation.

When he walked outside, Ruth turned to me. "We're going to get killed. What are you doing?" The cashier, who had heard the entire exchange, was listening intently.

"Ruth, I know it seems crazy and even reckless, but it really is okay. I'm sure that it's a genuine offer. I've been here long enough to know that people will genuinely offer help when they see the need. It's not like New York. And besides, we will drive in your car, they can follow in their truck. What's the worst that happens? They take off with the workbench."

The cashier smiled and reassured Ruth: "He's just being a good neighbor, dear. I think you're okay." And with that, we pushed the hand truck out of Home Depot and looked for the pickup truck.

A white truck pulled up and the young man climbed out of

the cab. I walked over and saw a fiftysomething-year-old woman seated in the passenger seat. "This is my mom," he said matter-of-factly. I introduced myself and Ruth and we loaded the workbench into the back of his truck.

Once at Ruth's place, he helped us unload the workbench and then offered to put it together. I could feel Ruth tensing up, but I knew it would be a bear to assemble with just the two of us. I asked his name. It was Robert. "That's really nice of you, Robert, but I wouldn't want to put your mom and you out any more than we already have."

"Oh, it's no trouble, ma'am. We don't have nowhere important to go. My mom don't mind."

"Okay, then," I said. "Thank you, Robert. Let's work on it out here."

He and Ruth began taking the parts out of the cardboard box and laying them in the grassy front yard one by one. Truth is, I didn't want to let him into Ruth's place—I had shed some of my New York cynicism, but I hadn't lost my mind.

As they started to build the bench, I walked over to the truck, thinking I might chat with his mom. I had two children of my own and thought it would be nice to compliment her on how generous her son was. There is nothing moms love more than hearing about the goodness of their children.

"Looks like the young folks are going to spend a little time building the workbench. I can't thank you enough. Your son is a lovely young man," I said. It was then that I noticed the army-green T-shirt she was wearing: TRUMP FOR PRESIDENT.

Oy vey, I thought to myself. *Serves me right.* The woman looked me up and down. "Hop on in," she said. "It's getting chilly out there."

I climbed up into the truck and we began to chat about small things—the tiles they had bought for their house, the weather (in Oklahoma, weather is a frequent topic of conversation), and the upcoming Halloween holiday. Niceties out of the way, she asked where I was from and what I was doing in Oklahoma. *Here goes*, I thought. I explained that I was from New York and had moved here to start a public defender office for women in the criminal justice system. I went on for a bit too long, nervous that when I stopped talking, I would have to endure a tirade of conservative rhetoric about crime, law enforcement, and the need to make people who "do the crime" "do the time." She barely took a breath before turning to me, looking me directly in the eyes, and saying: "Well, then you came here to do G-d's work."

Everything about the way I viewed the world was changing. I was constantly surprised by Oklahomans. Just when I wanted to put them in a box, they surprised me. Sometimes people I would meet who seemed progressive, or at least liberal enough, would suddenly drop what one of our lawyers called the "Oklahoma bomb." Typically, it would be a statement that exposed underlying racism, sexism, or just closed-mindedness. But then there were moments like this one in that white pickup truck, when I assumed Robert's mom would peg me for the blue-state, left-leaning ex-hippie that I was and dismiss me or be repulsed by my work. Her response encouraged me. So I went there.

After thanking her for her gracious comment about the work Still She Rises had set out to do, I asked: "Do you mind me asking why you support Donald Trump? How do you think that Trump becoming president would be beneficial to you or your family?"

Without hesitating, she went on to explain that she had five members of her family who had enlisted and been sent to Afghanistan and Iraq over the years. They were traumatized, and her husband was so badly injured that he needed a wheelchair. She railed not against the U.S. government that had decided to send her family members there but against the VA, which, in her opinion, had failed every member of her family. "Government doesn't work," she concluded. "And Trump is going to shake things up."

I was humbled into silence for a moment. My son was in his twenties, and all of his friends were as well. The notion that a single one of them would wind up in Iraq or Afghanistan was incomprehensible. They had privilege, access, and families that could support them into adulthood without their having to throw their bodies into a war for a chance at a career. She broke the silence by explaining that Robert was "different" from her other boys and he couldn't enlist. She went on, "He's hardworking, though, willing to do anything for anyone. He earns a little money by cutting down tree branches for neighbors up near where we live. Sometimes he will see a tree that needs trimming and go knock on their door and ask if he can cut the tree for them. I think he likes climbing up trees, like a monkey," she joked.

It was getting dark, and the temperature was dropping. Ruth

and Robert were finished putting the workbench together. They stood there chatting, satisfied with the work they had done getting all the pieces together.

"Robert, why don't you help the young lady and bring that into her apartment," his mother said. Without missing a beat, Ruth replied, "That would be great!" Somewhere between that checkout line at Home Depot and this moment, Ruth had determined that these were decent folks with good hearts who were just trying to help. I reached over and hugged Robert's mom, thanking her for her son and her graciousness and wishing her and her family well. I meant every word.

I got out of the truck and followed Ruth and Robert as they went into the building. Ruth directed us to her apartment and unlocked the door, and the two of them walked in, placing the workbench exactly where we had envisioned it. It was perfect. Ruth thanked Robert and I walked him out into the hall, promising Ruth that I'd be right back.

Once out in the hallway, I pulled out the twenty-dollar bill that I had been keeping in my pocket and offered it to him. "Robert, thank you so much for your time. We really appreciate it." He looked struck by my offer and began to shake his head. "No, ma'am," he said, "you don't need to give me nothing."

Realizing that I had insulted his good intentions, I tried again. "I know that you didn't want me to pay you for your time. I really appreciate that. It was so kind of you. But I would be so grateful if you would allow me to at least give you this money to help pay for the gas that you and your mom used to get us here.

It would mean a lot to me if you would allow me to show you my appreciation."

He hesitated, then agreed, tucking the twenty into his pocket. "Can I ask you for a favor?" he said. Fearful that he was about to ask me for Ruth's number, I said, "Sure, what can I do?" He handed me a small scrap of paper with blue ink on it. "My sister, ma'am, she's in prison. We don't get to see her too often. It's too hard on my mom to visit her there. That's her name and where she's at. Could you check on her and make sure she's okay?" I promised that I would, gave him a hug, and thanked him again for his help.

As I watched him climb into the truck next to his mother, I found myself overwhelmed and slightly confused. It's amazing how the things we tell ourselves about others can change when we genuinely listen to their stories. Someone can transform from an abstract caricature into a human being. Perhaps for the first time, I was beginning to apply to the world around me some of the same principles that allowed me to care and fight for people in the criminal justice system no matter what they were accused of.

Criminal justice reform might be stuck in a partisan divide, but mass incarceration does not care about party affiliation. Somewhere in the Great Plains of Oklahoma, their sister and daughter sat in a concrete cell behind bars, forgotten by society but not by the family she left behind. And that's the human story at the heart of criminal justice reform.

A few weeks later, I was driving down the highway in Tulsa

when I saw a huge billboard for a gun show at the local fairgrounds. I couldn't resist and took the exit.

Oddly, I know how to hold, load, and shoot a gun. I learned it as a kid. But I wasn't there to buy a gun. I was there because I was curious. I pulled into the massive parking lot and made my way to the entrance.

Walking into the huge, cavernous hall, I saw table after table, row after row, with every imaginable gun—long-barreled guns, small handguns, even brightly painted guns adorned with jewels. It was an incredible display of weaponry from one end of the hall to the other. I stopped to chat with some of the sellers. Everyone was happy to talk about what they were selling, and when I gently asked why they thought that I should have a gun, most explained that I should have a gun because there are "bad people out there and you have to be ready for them."

But guns weren't the only things for sale. As I turned a corner, I was startled to see a red flag with a big swastika on it hanging from one of the tables. Covering the tabletop was Nazi memorabilia of all types—arm patches, copies of Hitler's *Mein Kampf*, daggers with the Iron Cross, and other Third Reich paraphernalia. I wanted to be curious and ask questions about what motivated the merchant's interest in items related to the genocidal regime of Adolf Hitler, but I couldn't quite get there, so I walked by without saying a word. Perhaps this was a bridge too far even for me—at least for now. Compassion is certainly a journey.

9

What We've Done versus Who We Are

The year was 1993 and the man before me stood accused of murdering his fiancée. According to the police and medical examiner's reports, as his fiancée lay sleeping, Hector got up from the bed they shared, took a large kitchen knife, and, without warning, cut her throat so deeply that she was almost decapitated. Then, perched upright on his knees next to her body, he forced the knife into his own abdomen and pulled the handle to the right to disembowel himself. As their blood pooled together in the mattress, Hector curled up next to his dead fiancée, put his arms around her body, and waited to die. According to the report from the fire department, he had started a fire before he turned the knife on himself, hoping that the entire apartment and their bodies would go up in flames together.

In my life as a public defender, there were many times when I wholeheartedly believed in my client's innocence. Then my job was straightforward—to keep the burden of proof on the prosecution and defend my client's rights and freedom at all costs. There were also times when my client was guilty but the crime itself was the result of people in positions of power deciding to criminalize some things, and some people, and not others. Drug-related offenses, crimes of poverty, the criminalization of mental illness—all offenses that prosecutors ruthlessly targeted Black and brown communities for, filling America's jails with people who should have never stepped foot in the criminal justice system in the first place. In these cases, it was critical to defend clients zealously but also put the whole system on trial.

And then there were those clients who stood accused of heinous acts and, in fact, had committed them. They were the ones who always made me the most curious. Their stories called into question my own beliefs about justice and the possibility of compassion. In these cases, all I could do was seek to understand the person behind the act, show their humanity, and use every tactic in the book to mitigate their suffering.

Hector was one of those clients.

In the fire that night, he survived. The smoke drew the attention of his neighbors, who called the police, and it didn't take long for the fire department to arrive at the building, race up the six flights of stairs to the smoldering apartment, and enter the grotesque scene.

They found Hector in bed, half dead, moaning and cradling his fiancée's body, softly repeating, "I'm sorry . . . I'm sorry . . . I'm sorry." He was rushed to the hospital, where, overriding his clear desire to die, the doctors saved his life. He was twenty-five.

As I stood across from him in a small, cold cement room at Rikers Island, I wondered what could possibly explain his actions that night. The fact that he was guilty of a gruesome murder was indisputable, but this didn't answer the most important question: *Why?*

Years as a public defender had taught me that people don't wake up one day and decide to commit horrendous violence. There is always a context, a history, experiences that pave the path to doing the unthinkable.

This isn't to say that an individual shouldn't be held accountable when they commit harm. An explanation is not an excuse. But the story of how someone came to be, or act, can make meaning. Meaning is the soil of our common humanity, and recognizing that shared humanity is a path, however obscure, to redemption. Meaning provides *a way back*. Sometimes that is all you can fight for.

Hector was tall, shy, and gentle. He said hello softly and offered his hand for me to shake. I introduced myself, shook his hand, and asked him to sit down. For the next hour, we talked about a lot of things, but I carefully steered away from the evening he killed his fiancée and tried to end his life. I knew we had to go there eventually, but first I needed to establish trust.

Hector had no history of violence. He had never been arrested before and he had absolutely no idea what lay ahead. I spent a good deal of time explaining the legal process to him. He took it all in, asking questions when he needed more information. When I asked him to tell me more about himself, he talked about growing up in East Harlem with a large, loving family. He was raised in a public housing development, where he lived with his mother and grandparents. His mother was still alive, but his grandparents were both deceased. He went to the local public schools and performed well academically. He had no history of behavioral problems as a student, and after graduating from high school, he got a job in a video store, where he worked his way up until he was promoted to store manager.

Without going into the night of the events, I decided to ask about his fiancée, Luisa. He described her as smart, beautiful, and full of joy. He explained that they knew each other for several years and had recently gotten engaged. He was excited about the engagement and looking forward to being her husband and, eventually, a parent with her. But as the conversation continued, he got quieter and began to look away from me.

"Hector, can you tell me what happened that night at the apartment? I know it's hard, but I would really like to understand what happened. Do you think you can tell me?"

He looked up at me. "I was laying there and thinking about it all. We were engaged. I kept looking at the ring I gave her. I loved her so much . . ."

"I can see that, Hector," I said. "Can you tell me more about what happened?"

"She was cheating on me. Or I think she was. My mind was just racing. I couldn't stop thinking about it. I kept imagining it." He paused. "But I don't remember doing anything. I don't remember hurting her."

His shock and confusion seemed genuine.

There was an easy explanation right in front of me. He suspected Luisa was cheating on him, and in a jealous rage, he killed her. For most prosecutors that would have been the end of the inquiry. They had the facts and now they had the intent. But for some reason, it didn't satisfy me. There I was, a feminist who had written papers about misogynistic violence against women, more curious about this man's experience than about the woman he had killed.

Hector began sobbing uncontrollably with his head in his hands. I sat silently. There was nothing to say. I watched as the weight of what happened began to fall upon him. It was as if the events of that night were finally making their way through the haze of shock and denial and into his consciousness. The recognition of what he had done was crushing him before my eyes, and all I could do was sit there quietly as his world crumbled.

A corrections officer signaled that our time was almost up. Hector tried to push back the emotional tidal wave and regain his composure. I touched his hand and reassured him that I would be back. I asked if there was anything he needed from me before I left. "Can you end this nightmare?" he replied.

"I wish I could, Hector." I meant it with every bone in my body. "I'll see you soon." And with that, I left.

Over the next six months, I thought about Hector regularly. There were the routine court dates where we saw each other, and several motions to be filed on his behalf with the court, but that wasn't why he was on my mind so often. I was struggling to make sense of what he had done and why my mind rejected a simple explanation. Something was missing, but I couldn't for the life of me figure out what it was. In an attempt to find out more, I hired a well-known psychiatrist to visit Hector at Rikers Island and do a full psychosocial evaluation of him. Maybe the doctor would uncover what I could only intuit. I wasn't sure, but it was worth a try.

As expected, things on the legal front were not going well. The prosecutor explained that the only offer available to Hector was pleading guilty to the highest charge and getting the maximum sentence. In other words, Hector had no offer. The prosecutor had a slam-dunk case, an outraged father of the victim who came to every single court date, and indisputable facts. This was, in his words, exactly the kind of case you spend your resources prosecuting. Making matters worse, we were in front of a judge who routinely handed out harsh sentences and showed little mercy. The prosecutor and judge knew that I didn't have a lot of bargaining room, and so did I.

The psychiatrist visited Hector many times over the next few months. After each visit, I hoped the psychiatrist would call, that maybe this time he would have a revelation and finally give me an explanation, a diagnosis, anything that would help make sense of what had happened. Maybe the psychiatrist would discover that Hector was hearing voices and had undiagnosed schizophrenia, or that he had been in a drug-induced psychotic state. Anything. But the psychiatrist had no answers.

I went back to the drawing board to try to find an answer myself.

I visited with Hector as often as I could and got to know him and his family well. With every visit and every interaction, I formed a fuller picture of him. He was smart, kind, and humble. He worked hard and shared his earnings with family members who needed help.

Hector made no excuses for what he had done, but he seemed as baffled by the facts as the people who knew him. He likened it to a dream that made no sense, a dream where he could not recognize himself. Yet its reality was undeniable. He was filled with guilt and ready to accept whatever punishment came his way.

Luisa's father attended every court date, and you could feel his pain and rage fill the room. Hector always emerged the same way from the back of the courtroom, handcuffed and flanked by guards, his head down, avoiding eye contact with Luisa's father at all costs.

The father's hatred wasn't reserved for Hector alone. Whenever our eyes met, I could feel his rage directed at me for representing the man who killed his daughter. As a defense attorney, this is a feeling you grow used to. At the time, I was pregnant with my second child, and the full term would take us to the eve of trial. I remember thinking about the child growing inside me as I bore witness to another parent's unimaginable pain.

As I started to prepare for trial, I still had no idea why Hector had done what he did that night. My only avenue of defense was to convince the jury of what I believed—that it wasn't an intentional murder but instead a manslaughter that was driven by an irrational, spontaneous moment and without forethought. A conviction for manslaughter would reduce the twenty-five-to-life sentence that Hector would surely get on a murder conviction to only eight and a third to twenty-five years.

In preparing for the trial, I interviewed several members of Hector's family. Their accounts only echoed the shock and disbelief that Hector himself had felt when he became aware of what he had done.

But all families have skeletons in the closet. And one day that closet door opened.

"You know, it's strange that this happened after what happened to his grandmother," an aunt said in passing, almost as an afterthought.

"What do you mean?" I asked. "What happened to his grandmother?"

She shared that when Hector was around five years old, his grandfather killed his grandmother, stabbing her over twenty times. He had suspected her of having feelings for another man. I was speechless. Hector had never told me the story, either because it was buried so deep that he couldn't remember or because he didn't see the connection.

Then Hector's aunt informed me that in the weeks leading up to Luisa's murder, Hector had learned something that shook the very foundation of his life and identity. The father whom he loved turned out not to be his father. His mother had cheated on him with another man. The family had closed ranks and kept the secret from him.

I went over these stories over and over again in my mind. I imagined how his grandmother's gruesome murder must have haunted Hector, clinging to him like a second skin, a deep trauma that he wore silently, subconsciously, until the truth about his own mother transformed it into a single moment of uncontrollable rage. And so in the dark of night, in a nightmare of his own making, he replicated what his grandfather had done all those years ago.

This wasn't a legal justification for the murder, or even a mitigating factor for sentencing, but when I discussed these events with Hector, it seemed to help him make sense of that fateful night. He wasn't a monster, even though he had committed a monstrous crime. He was a victim of his own trauma and, on that night, a victimizer.

There are no movie villains in real life. Often, trauma and pain fuel our actions. Sometimes it is familial. Sometimes it is the trauma that a community has experienced historically that can trigger a destructive response. None of us is immune from that possibility, but only some of us—the privileged, wealthy, and, mostly, white—have access to the resources, support, and therapy we need to process devastating experiences so that they don't control our futures.

Hearing these stories about Hector's life and seeing Hector

process this trauma filled me with profound sadness. What does justice even mean in the face of such a tragedy for all involved? What meaning does guilt or innocence even hold when a person is the victim of their own trauma? I know the blunt answers that our criminal justice system offers to these complex questions, but I also know our children deserve better.

The trial began. I was nearly nine months pregnant with my soon-to-be daughter, barely able to get in or out of cabs, but ready to give the jury my best.

The prosecutor intended to admit into evidence photographs of the crime scene, including pictures of the shocking and grotesque injuries. They were enough to make anyone sick to their stomach. We wanted to keep them out of evidence—we weren't challenging the manner of death, or the fact that Hector was the one who did it—but the prosecutor knew there was no better way to inflame the jury, and the judge allowed it.

The photos were going to come in, so we spent time thinking about how we could best prepare the jury for them, inoculate them as best we could, so that the sight of all that blood and all that violence didn't cloud their ability to hear our defense. It was a tall order.

We planned to introduce the evidence of Hector's attempted suicide in graphic detail to counter the prosecution. While it was an admission of guilt on the one hand, it was also evidence of his extreme emotional state at the time. We hoped the jury would recognize that anyone capable of plunging a knife into their abdomen and then cutting away at their own internal organs was incapable of rational thought. That was key to convincing them that he was under "extreme emotional disturbance" that night—a mitigating rather than exculpatory defense specific to New York State law that we hoped would reduce the murder to a manslaughter.

Luisa's father sat in the second row of the courtroom, clearly visible to the jurors and making no effort to hide his contempt and rage. Sitting through the days of testimony that came next must have been excruciating for him. At one point, he had to leave the courtroom when the medical examiner was describing the injuries that caused her death. His pain was unimaginable to me. I tried to stop myself from even thinking about it. Sitting next to Hector through that testimony, I could feel his body tense up at every detail until he leaned over and told me that he thought he was going to be sick to his stomach. I quickly asked for a break. The judge couldn't turn me down, since he had gone out of his way at the start of the trial to say that if I needed any extra breaks because of my "condition," he would be happy to accommodate me. "After all," he said, "I don't want you having that baby in my courtroom."

The trial lasted only a week. The night before summations were scheduled to begin, I began having mild contractions in the small Middle Eastern restaurant where my colleagues and I had gathered to discuss what I was going to say the next day. "Don't worry," I reassured them as I began to furiously jot down notes on the paper napkins on the table. "Let's write this down now, and if I can't make it to court tomorrow, you've got this."

They looked terrified, but we were in this bunker together

and they knew what they had to do. We finished up, paid the check, and said good night. I sneaked quietly into my apartment, not wanting to wake my husband or three-year-old son. I took a hot shower to clear my mind and rehearse my argument. Then I climbed into bed. As I lay there, I imagined Hector in the dark cell, alone with his thoughts, resigned to his fate while still wrestling with the reality of what he had done. Somewhere between falling asleep and waking up at three in the morning, the contractions stopped. I was ready for the closing statement.

Pacing back and forth in front of the jury, my big belly covered by the peacock-blue maternity blouse I had bought for the trial, I did everything I could to persuade the jurors to consider a lesser charge. They were attentive and I could see that they were considering my arguments carefully. In the end, they stayed out for two days deliberating, a sign that they didn't think this was a slam-dunk case and genuinely considered the bigger picture.

By the end of a trial, most defense lawyers have convinced themselves that they are going to win. By then, you believe in your story, your client, and the facts as you see them. I was no exception. I allowed myself to believe the jury would convict Hector of the lesser count and, in doing so, grant him the possibility of someday being free again. I should have known better. I was asking them for understanding, not forgiveness, but it was naive to think that understanding alone could lead to compassion. They found him guilty of murder and sealed his fate.

Hector had long accepted the debt he had to pay. And while it tortured him that he would never be able to take back what he had done, it was clear that learning about and accepting his trauma allowed him to reclaim himself. I knew that he was so much more than the violence he committed that night, and so did he.

After the verdict was read, the jury was excused. We sat in silence as the judge set a sentencing date. Hector told me to take care of myself and my baby. We hugged and I watched as he was escorted by the court officers into the jail cell at the back of the courtroom. He would be picked up and taken to Rikers Island to await sentencing.

My daughter, Emma, was born the following week. Soon after, I returned for the sentencing hearing. Despite my arguments for a lesser sentence of fifteen to life, the judge gave him the maximum allowable by law—twenty-five years to life in prison. Luisa's father watched from the back of the courtroom as the judge administered the sentence. I wondered if it brought him closure or lessened his suffering in any way.

Every year, I calculate Hector's time in prison with my daughter's birthday. Twenty-seven years and counting. In my thoughts, I see him as a five-year-old boy. I see his innocence cursed. I see the torrent of pain and confusion as he looked over at Luisa in her sleep that fateful night. And I see him in a prison cell, almost three decades after his conviction, and wonder what possible purpose there could be in holding him there any longer.

Undoing mass incarceration will require a fundamental reorientation of the criminal justice system. Matters of poverty, health, and racial inequity must be addressed through social policies and investments rather than entrenched through criminalization. This is common sense if we aspire to live in a society where all can thrive.

But reimagining justice is an altogether different task. Justice is exercised and experienced at the individual level, where social and historical contexts might explain, but do not excuse, a person's actions. Retribution and vengeance are powerful forces in our society and thus the criminal justice system. A historical understanding of how we got to this point might help us end the policies and politics that weaponize the criminal justice system against entire communities of people, but only the inner work of compassion can change what we expect from justice when individuals commit harm.

Compassion begins when we accept that we are more than our own worst moment. It is an important lesson—though by no means an easy one—that you understand when you love individuals who are deeply flawed or when you yourself have been judged on the basis of a single act.

For me, learning how to represent people at precisely that time in their lives—their own worst moment—taught me this lesson. I don't think it is our natural human inclination to think this way, and our criminal justice system certainly does not encourage it, but it has served me well, not only in my personal relationships but also in becoming an effective advocate for those I defended in court. I also think it's a better way to be in this world.

10

Skin in the Game versus a Pound of Flesh

The phone rings in the middle of the night. It's your frightened seventeen-year-old son, who has been arrested and is in police custody. He tells you that someone accused him of stealing a backpack, but he swears he didn't do it. Then you learn that a judge set bail in the amount of $3,000. Unless you can pay it in the next few hours, he will be transferred to a massive jail complex known for its violence and appalling conditions, where he will stay until his trial date.

If you have the money, you rush to the precinct to pay the bail and start calling friends to get recommendations for the best criminal defense lawyer in town. But what if you don't have $3,000? Indeed, what if you don't even have $300 to pay the 10 percent fee to hire a bail bonds agent to be the surety? You wouldn't be alone. Nearly 40 percent of Americans don't have $400 in savings for an emergency expense.[1] So what would you do?

In 2010, this is what happened to Venida Browder. Her son, Kalief, was seventeen years old when he was accused of stealing a backpack. When Venida could not afford his $3,000 bail, Kalief was transferred to Rikers Island. As mothers often do, Venida tried to find a way. She borrowed money from a neighbor to hire a bondsman, hoping that would bring him home, but Kalief's arrest triggered a probation violation from a prior case, and the court would not release him. As a result, he sat at Rikers Island for three years while his case worked its way through the court system. While his friends lived out their high school years and graduated, Kalief was beaten, bullied, and thrown into solitary confinement. He maintained his innocence the entire time.

After three years of pretrial incarceration, Kalief's case was completely dismissed. In 2015, he committed suicide. The next year, his grieving mother, Venida, died of a heart attack.

On May 25, 2018, in a courthouse not far from where Kalief was arraigned, a judge set bail of $1 million for Harvey Weinstein after the movie mogul was arrested on charges of rape and sexual abuse. Mr. Weinstein showed up to his arraignment with one of the city's top defense lawyers by his side and a cashier's check made out for the full bail amount. He surrendered his passport and agreed to wear an ankle monitor. The whole process took about an hour. Mr. Weinstein was chauffeured back to his mansion to await trial. The rest is history.

I'm not suggesting Mr. Weinstein should have been sent to jail to await trial. Indeed, the conditions of release in this case were reasonable to ensure he could be at liberty until proved guilty, while mitigating the risk that he might flee the jurisdiction to escape prosecution.

Surely there were conditions of release that could have allowed seventeen-year-old Kalief to remain home with his mother, but they were never considered, unlike in Mr. Weinstein's case.

All too often the presumption of innocence is a privilege afforded only to those who can pay bail. For the poor in America, if you can't pay, you remain in jail as if you had been found guilty already.

Our Constitution promises equal justice under the law, so how did we end up with a two-tier system where money buys due process?

After all, we appear to have all the right tools to operate a fair system and ensure that everyone has an equal shot at defending themselves against an unproved accusation:

- The law presumes you innocent.

- The burden of proof is on the prosecution.

- You have a right to counsel, and if you can't afford one, you are entitled to a free public defender.

- You have a right to a speedy trial.

- There are strict rules of evidence that must be followed to prove any given fact.

The list goes on.

The whole package is fundamental to the health of a democracy and the rule of law. It is a robust system—and we could be proud of it—except what's on paper doesn't match how the system operates in practice. Nowhere is this clearer than when it comes to bail.

I can still remember the night we got the phone call. I must have been in middle school then. My mother was seated at the Formica counter in our long, narrow kitchen, smoking a Salem menthol cigarette and glancing at a magazine. I knew right away something was terribly wrong. It's not that disturbing late-night phone calls were unusual in our house. The women my father had affairs with, people we owed money to, or just family and friends concerned that my father had disappeared again—those calls happened more often than I could count, but I had a gut feeling this was different. I pretended that I was doing homework, but I could see the tension on my mother's face and hear the panic in her voice. "Okay," she said, "what happens now? Will he be able to come home? How much?"

That was the first time I heard about cash bail. My father had been arrested for a serious felony and was in police custody. A judge had set bail. Unless we could pay, he would remain in jail until the case was decided. It was an odd notion even for a kid. Why money? What if you didn't have grandparents who could help you out?

Years earlier, Bobby Kennedy, then the U.S. attorney general, addressed the Senate Judiciary Committee and explained:

[The] problem, simply stated is: the rich man and the poor man do not receive equal justice in our courts. And in no area is this more evident than in the matter of bail. . . . [Bail] has become a vehicle for systematic injustice. Every year in this country, thousands of persons are kept in jail for weeks and even months following arrest. They are not yet proven guilty. They may be no more likely to flee than you or I. But, nonetheless, most of them must stay in jail because, to be blunt, they cannot afford to pay for their freedom.[2]

Since then, the misuse of bail has only become more widespread in the American criminal justice system, leading to more and more inequitable results.

By the time I became a public defender in the early eighties, we were well on our way to mass incarceration and bail was driving a dramatic increase in the number of people held in jails before trial, as well as racial disparities. The problem has only gotten worse. Since the 1970s, the number of people held pretrial has increased by 433 percent.[3] Today, on any given night, more than half a million people go to sleep in jail cells across the U.S. without having been convicted of a crime.[4]

It wasn't always this way.

The original idea behind bail was simple. When you are accused of a crime and brought to court, the judge must decide whether you can go free while the case is pending or whether you should be held in jail pretrial. If the judge decides to let you go home, they can either release you on a promise that you will return to court as needed (release on recognizance) or require you to put up money—bail—that you lose if you flee. Bail was intended to create some "skin in the game," not de facto detention if you are poor.

However, for bail to work as intended, it must be affordable. That is why the U.S. Constitution explicitly prohibits excessive bail. Additionally, the Supreme Court has stated that "[in] our society, liberty is the norm, and detention prior to trial or without trial is the carefully limited exception."[5] Today, nothing could be further from the truth. Pretrial detention is the norm.

Judges ought to take these words to heart and make decisions about pretrial detention in a careful, thoughtful manner. Instead, they routinely set bail with little or no regard for one's ability to pay, making detention before trial (for the poor) the norm rather than the exception.

You may be thinking, *Well, don't do the crime if you can't do the time.* But remember that bail is set at the very beginning of a case, meaning no evidence has been presented yet. There is only an unproved accusation. Most bail hearings last only a few minutes. There are virtually no legal arguments or questioning of witnesses. There is no opportunity to tell the judge your side of the story. It's a perfunctory process designed for one purpose only—to process you into or out of jail while your case is pending.

When we talk about ending cash bail, we're not saying there should be no accountability for crimes. All we're saying is that the treatment you receive before adjudication, while you are still presumed innocent, should not depend on the size of your wallet.

Moreover, the misuse of bail to lock up poor people before conviction costs us all.

It costs us economically. American taxpayers spend about $40 million a day to incarcerate people awaiting trial. That's $14 billion each year—enough to fund salaries for more than a quarter of a million elementary school teachers. Factor in the collateral costs to families and society at large, and the price tag of pretrial detention in the U.S. is closer to $140 billion annually.[6]

It costs us socially. About two thirds of people passing through our jails are dealing with issues of mental health or drug addiction.[7] Rather than receiving access to treatment and care, they remain in jail because they cannot afford bail. Moreover, bail tears families apart and causes irreparable harm and loss.

And it costs us morally. Bail erodes due process and exacerbates inequality. There is also ample evidence of systemic racism in bail practices. Judges are more likely to set cash bail if you are Black or brown, and the bail amount will be higher than that set for your white counterpart charged with the same offense.[8]

Simply put, cash bail corrupts justice.

As a public defender I have stood next to thousands of people as they were hauled off to jail because a judge knowingly set cash bail that was unaffordable. Sometimes that bail was imposed out of habit and indifference, like the time my client, a young mother of three, was held in jail on $500 bail, accused of stealing Tylenol out of a local drugstore. When I argued that she could not afford it because she was working at a minimum-wage job and was already on the economic edge, the judge responded dispassionately that it wasn't his problem and called the next case.

Sometimes cash bail was set by judges because they could not see beyond the scary nature of the accusation.

Early on in my career, I represented a Latino teenager charged with murder. Sergio was barely five foot four, wore thick glasses, and loved Russian novels. The facts were not in dispute: He woke up in the middle of the night to loud noises coming from the living room of the top-floor, rent-controlled apartment he shared with his mother and siblings in the Bronx. Thinking there was an intruder in the house, he grabbed the rifle his family kept hidden in the hallway closet for protection and headed straight for the living room. There, in the dark among the shadows, Sergio could see his stepfather standing over his mother, one hand gripping her neck, the other holding a baseball bat. The previous night, there had been a terrible fight between them that left his mother badly bruised and battered. Afterward, she had thrown her husband out of the house, but now he was back to get his revenge.

Standing in the hall doorway, gun in hand pointing directly at his stepfather, Sergio told him to get out. His stepfather sneered at him and with a slight smile said, "Oh yeah, tough guy, what are you doing to do about it?" Sergio pulled the trigger. As he would describe it to me later, sobbing inside his jail cell, the next thing he knew his stepfather was on the ground, bleeding to death on the brown shag carpet that covered the family's living room floor.

Sergio was arrested and charged with murder. At his bail hearing, the courtroom was packed with family members pleading for his release. We submitted medical records that proved in gory detail the extensive history of domestic abuse Sergio's mother had suffered at the hands of the deceased. Friends, family, and high school teachers submitted letters attesting to Sergio's gentle nature and bright future. His mother, tears rolling down her face, begged the judge to release him to her custody while he awaited trial. "I lost my husband. Please don't take my child from me," she pleaded.

There was no reason to hold Sergio in jail before trial. He wasn't going anywhere. His entire world was in the Bronx, and he had a loving family ready to support him. He was not a danger to anyone else. His actions that night were clearly in defense of his mother's life, and he was ready to take responsibility for them. But the judge didn't see him that way. Focusing only on the nature of the charge, he set bail at $50,000, knowing that the family would never be able to afford it. The case took over two years of plea bargaining to get to its conclusion. In the end, the prosecutor offered Sergio a sentence of probation.

For a moment, imagine you are the one facing an accusation. The police arrest you. Perhaps you are innocent. Perhaps you did something, but it's not as serious as the allegation says. After all, it's not uncommon for prosecutors to overcharge at first so that later they can offer you a plea bargain to the lesser, more accurate charge and avoid the hassle and expense of a trial.[9] So they bring you to court, where you meet your lawyer just a few minutes before appearing in front of the judge. Before you even get the chance to explain yourself, cash bail is set. You can't afford it. You call friends and family to ask for help, but no one has that much cash or even enough collateral to get a bondsman.

Unable to pay your bail, you are brought to jail, where you are stripped, searched, and given an inmate number. You are escorted to your cell—an eight-by-twelve-foot cement box with a single metal bed, a toilet out in the open, and a small window high on the wall, the only connection you have to the outside world.

There is constant noise. The sounds of other prisoners, guards yelling, metal doors banging, and security buzzers going off at all hours make it impossible to fully rest. Inedible food is doled out on plastic trays, exercise is limited to walking around in a metal cage, and even your most personal hygiene routines are on public display in the jail's communal showers and toilets. You don't know whom to trust, and the ever-present threat of violence fills you with fear every hour.

Your life is falling apart. Your boss has already left several voice mails asking why you have not come to work. Your children are now living with different family members and keep asking where you are. You haven't had your blood pressure medication since you were arrested. No one can take care of your dog. Rent and utilities are overdue. There is no end in sight.

Now, imagine a few weeks go by and someone offers you a way out. Just plead guilty and we'll sentence you to the time you've already done in jail. It will be over. Granted, you will end up with a criminal record, but you can go home. What would you do? How long would you sit in jail just for the chance to tell your side of the story? Given the choices, almost everyone pleads guilty, whether they did it or not. That is why cash bail is perhaps the single most coercive lever that judges and prosecutors have at their fingertips to get a guilty plea.

I have long thought that before anyone is allowed to become a judge and hear criminal cases, they should have to spend at least twenty-four hours in a jail cell. Not because I am sadistic but because it might bring them just a little closer to understanding how terrifying and upending the experience of jail is, even for a short amount of time, and why people in that situation so readily forfeit their presumption of innocence and right to a trial. The experience might make a judge think twice before setting unaffordable cash bail. It might even give them a little courage.

On countless nights, I lay awake thinking about the rank unfairness of cash bail. In those moments, I even fantasized about becoming a judge myself so I could shake things up by refusing to set cash bail. Then I would remind myself that if I tried that, the powers that be would likely throw me off the criminal bench in no time, relegating me to traffic court for the rest of my life. No black polyester robes for me.

Then one night, what started as a venting session about the issue turned into a plan. My husband, David, a career public defender who never fails to see injustice, asked me, "What if we just started posting the damn bails?"

Since the bail payment comes back to the person who paid it once the criminal case ends—regardless of guilt or innocence—why couldn't we collect donations and build a "revolving" bail fund to provide free bail assistance to our clients? Assuming people came back to court, the money would keep recycling and we could use it to help other people, thus creating a self-sustaining fund.

It was David's ingenious idea, but like so many things in the give-and-take of our many decades of friendship and later marriage, I made it happen. We called it the Bronx Freedom Fund.

The year was 2005, and raising money to start something like this was more than challenging. Criminal justice reform was not a hot topic in philanthropy back then. Indeed, it was barely talked about, period. Various organizations and communities over the years had raised bail funds for specific people or political movements.[10] But this was something different—a sustainable revolving fund designed to help complete strangers and funded by private philanthropic dollars for the purpose of leveling the playing field in the courthouse.

In fairness, it wasn't just the novelty of the idea that made it a hard sell for funders. There were also many unanswered questions. First among them was whether people would return to court if they did not have money on the line.

If money turned out to be the primary motivator for coming back to court, we would lose all the funders' money. But what if it turned out that money had nothing to do with it? What if people simply came back on their own because that's what they had to do? Not only could we create a sustainable way to free people while their cases were pending, but we would also be gathering indisputable evidence to demonstrate that money had no place in our justice system.

It took two years of knocking on doors before I found anyone willing to invest in our idea. Our first funder was Jason Flom, a music executive. He gave us a startup grant of $100,000 to start the Bronx Freedom Fund, and we were off and running.

In those early years, we encountered many obstacles, including an all-out legal war with a Bronx criminal court judge, who unsuccessfully tried to use his perch on the bench to shut us down. Despite that, with each passing day, we were learning more.

Did people return to court even though they had no financial "skin in the game"? Yes, and overwhelmingly. Over 95 percent returned, laying waste to the myth that without cash bail there is no incentive to show up to court. For the 5 percent who missed court at some point, the reasons were myriad, but it was rarely an attempt to avoid court. None of our clients were getting in their private jets to escape prosecution. We learned that the key was addressing the various practical obstacles that arise, like lack of transportation or missing a court notification because you don't have a permanent address. By providing free MetroCards, sending text reminders to let people know about their next court date, and troubleshooting when barriers like lack of childcare came up, the Bronx Freedom Fund maintained a high rate of return.

We also learned what public defenders and their clients knew all along—that cash bail ensures easy guilty pleas and quick case turnover. It is the oil that keeps the machine running. The data was indisputable. Over half of the people we bailed out in the Bronx had their cases dismissed entirely, and of the remainder, almost no one received a jail sentence. Freedom made all the difference.

After ten years, we decided to take this effort national. A village of friends, colleagues, and supporters helped me draft a proposal to scale our work that we submitted to TED's Audacious Project for funding. It was a long shot, and I never thought we would win. After all, we were trying to convince them to help us free tens of thousands of people from jails across America.

Remarkably, we got the grant, and with a small team sitting around my kitchen table, we launched the Bail Project in the fall of 2017. The plan was to expand to dozens of cities across America to provide free bail assistance, gather evidence that people returned to court, and use data, along with people's stories, to make the case for ending cash bail. Success would mean putting ourselves out of business.

In our first five years, the Bail Project freed over twenty-five thousand people in more than thirty jurisdictions across America— from New York to Mississippi to Oklahoma to California—and produced results similar to what we had seen in the Bronx. The proof was clear: cash bail is not only unfair but also unnecessary.

So why do we keep using it? What keeps driving us to incarcerate millions of people every year before they have been convicted of anything?

It's complicated. To start, there is just the inertia of how things "have always been done." It's hard to break ingrained judicial habits and courthouse culture. Then there are the powerful, entrenched interests in maintaining the status quo, like the $2–billion–a–year bail bond industry, which exists only because cash bail does. Making matters worse, our criminal justice system has become one of the largest employers in the country, so any move to downsize would be a struggle. And then there is something less obvious, less tangible. Bail has largely become a proxy for this powerful human force. It's fear.

If I have learned anything in the past forty years working to bring more fairness into the American criminal justice system, it is that the single biggest obstacle to progress is not bad policies but the fear that drives them.

Judges are uniquely afraid of winding up on the front page of their local newspaper for having released someone who goes out and commits a violent crime. Policy makers don't want to risk appearing "soft" on crime and getting drummed out of office. But they're not the only problem.

We all play a role in allowing our fears to drive policy. Maybe that's to be expected. After all, no one wants to be victimized, so we do what we think will protect us and our loved ones. In reality, violent crime is relatively rare. However, our fear of it is deep and wildly contagious.

The problem is that fear can be real, but not necessarily grounded in reality. Fear is so powerful an emotion that it overwhelms rationality and kills compassion. Sometimes the reaction to fear is to act decisively; other times it is to remain passive and silent. Either way, scare us enough, and we will do unimaginable things to *feel* safe again. Nowhere is that clearer than in the criminal justice context.

We become so scared that we turn the people who are charged with committing crimes into the imaginary monsters we feared as children. Label someone a monster, and anything can be done to them. We will justify the indefensible. The draconian criminal laws we pass, the frequently excessive sentences we inflict, the horrendous jail conditions we allow to exist, and the chronic abuse of cash bail are all responses to fear.

It is fear that prevents us from seeing someone charged with a crime as someone we can relate to, someone with a life story, a family, hopes and struggles, highs and lows—someone worthy of compassion. Instead, we see them as completely "other." We label them *criminals, inmates, felons, ex-offenders.* We tell ourselves there is no "us" in "them," just "us versus them." We lose sight of their full humanity, reducing them to a single moment, demonizing them, and then using jails and prisons to put them out of sight and out of mind, no matter the cost.

What is clear is that we have twisted our entire criminal justice system around our fears, and we all bear some responsibility for that. It's time to do better. But it will take courage.

11

Fear versus Courage

Our fears make us vulnerable: to misinformation, to fearmongering, and even to our own worst instincts.

Fear of strangers. Fear of an idea. Fear of loss of position. Fear of sudden change. Fear of harm. Fear of failure. Fear is the common denominator in every playbook that stops progress, including the current pushback against efforts to reform our criminal justice system.

During the past ten years, there has been a remarkable and long-overdue national reawakening to the reality of systemic racism in America and its manifestation in our criminal justice institutions. Mass demonstrations, grassroots organizing, incisive journalism, social media outrage, and action by big corporations (and even by a Kardashian) have paved the way for growing recognition of a problem that has suddenly become mainstream. People no longer look at me like I have two heads when I talk about overhauling criminal justice. Raising money for the types of projects I run has become easier. My kids' friends now think I'm cool. Things are changing, but not as deeply as we need them to.

Fear still wins the day.

The discourse about structural racism and the ills of mass incarceration is easy to grasp intellectually because the facts are indisputable, but reason doesn't always triumph in the face of crime. And fear is what ultimately drives our policies.

In the years leading up to 2020, overall crime rates in America remained near historic lows. Then the COVID-19 pandemic hit. It killed over one million Americans, shook the foundations of our society, ravaged the economy, and created mass uncertainty, anxiety, and isolation—a perfect storm that led to a surge in gun sales and violent crime. Simultaneously, mass demonstrations in the wake of the police killings of Breonna Taylor, George Floyd, and others called loudly and unanimously for criminal justice reform.

The media quickly saw an opportunity to fearmonger. News programs churned out story after story about the violent-crime surge. And the more people watched this crime-related content, the more their fear grew. Higher ratings incentivized networks to continue reporting crime stories night after night, and by 2022, over 50 percent of Americans reported that they personally worried a "great deal" about crime.[1]

While the impact of the pandemic on crime was evident, political opportunists exploited the moment by pinning the blame for rising crime rates on criminal justice reform even in places where no reforms had taken place. In the case of the Bail Project, critics blamed bail reform for increased crime rates across the nation, yet bail reform has been enacted in only a handful of jurisdictions to date, with only one state, Illinois, actually ending cash bail across the board (and its reforms won't even take effect until 2023). Despite no evidence of a causal relationship between bail reform and America's rising crime rates, the narrative took hold.[2]

Politicization of fear is used by both parties, and even in the most liberal of states. In California, for example, prosecutors who won on promises to end racial bias in criminal justice and advance policies for prevention and diversion rather than incarceration soon faced fierce opposition. In fact, San Francisco's progressive prosecutor Chesa Boudin, who was elected in 2020, was removed from office by recall before he could finish his first term. And in New York, even liberals called on their governor to roll back bail reform. Doubts about the wisdom of criminal justice reform permeated both parties.

Fear took hold, and suddenly the moral clarity that had ignited the mass protests for racial justice and reform began to fade everywhere, even among liberals and former supporters. That's how powerful fear can be.

To put these fears into perspective, let's talk about murder, the most serious crime. In 2022, the murder rate hit a high of 0.007 percent of the population as a result of the pandemic crime surge.[3]

If we are doing a pure risk analysis, the risk of fatal car crashes is nearly twice as high.[4] The risk of death by drug overdose is three times higher.[5] This is not to minimize or trivialize the harm caused when someone is murdered but rather to offer a rational, statistical context for our emotional responses.

In some ways, our national debate about criminal justice is like Groundhog Day 1988, every day, when Willie Horton became a household name.

Horton had committed a heinous crime during his release as part of a prison furlough program in Massachusetts. At the time, all fifty states had furlough programs that were actually quite successful, allowing incarcerated people a temporary release to tend to personal or family matters, such as receiving medical treatment, seeking future employment, or attending a funeral. However, a single thirty-second ad about Horton, run by George H. W. Bush during his presidential campaign, changed all that. The ad not only torpedoed the campaign of his opponent, Michael Dukakis, who had been the governor of Massachusetts at the time Horton was released. It also unleashed a panic and backlash across the nation that led several states to completely end their furlough programs and even eliminate parole for countless people.

The ad made the larger public afraid of releasing *anyone* before the end of their sentence, for fear of "another Willie Horton." Talk about the exception dictating the rule. In 1991, just weeks before his death from a brain tumor, Lee Atwater, the mastermind behind the Willie Horton campaign, reflected on his role:

"My illness helped me to see that what was missing in society is what was missing in me: a little heart, a lot of brotherhood."[6]

Since then, the Willie Horton effect has been deployed by Republicans and Democrats alike every time it's politically expedient. And for good reason. When it comes to crime, we lose perspective and are often unable to hold on to rational thought. We hear about someone committing a violent crime, and we get scared. That's understandable. We imagine ourselves, or someone we love, being the next victim. That triggers a response to do something—anything—to *feel* safe again. We generalize from the exception, then legislate around it. No more "dangerously lenient" parole. No more "soft" diversion programs handed out to repeat offenders. No more bail reform for those who haven't been convicted. Better safe than sorry.

Even when there is no evidence to support the position that jailing more people for longer stretches makes us any safer, it makes us *feel* safer. The fear we have of crime, and those who commit it, is so powerful that we have built entire systems around the exception, casting a wide net and impacting millions of people and entire communities. We use jails and prisons excessively not because it works but because it quells our fears. It's not rational. It's a salve.

If we are ever going to create rational and more effective criminal justice policy, decisions should be based on the rule rather than the exception, because even in the best-case scenarios there are always exceptions.

The overwhelming majority of Americans who are booked into jails every year are dealing with issues of drug addiction, mental illness, and crushing poverty.[7] We cannot incarcerate our way out of these social ills. We already tried that. The radical mass-incarceration experiment of the past four decades has not worked. As I've said before, if it had, we would be the safest nation in the world. We are quite the opposite. In fact, mass incarceration has exacerbated the very conditions that lead to more crime.

But we don't just fear crime. We demonize, ostracize, and dehumanize those who commit crime. Fear prevents us from separating what someone did in a moment from who they are and who they could become.

As I have encouraged you in previous chapters, imagine facing this type of judgment. Picture the most shameful thing you've ever done. Keep it to yourself, but now think about how it might feel to be defined by that act forever. Forget what came before that instant and ignore everything you have achieved since then. In the eyes of others, you are nothing more than that shameful moment. It feels unfair, doesn't it? Only you know if others would be right or wrong to fear or loathe you.

Fear blinds us to the humanity of others, and the flip side of fear is the silent cruelty of indifference. Jails and prisons create in our imagination the irredeemable "other." We ignore the larger social and economic issues that shape our lives and create conditions of safety and opportunity for some but not others. We judge a person's worth and life solely in light of their own worst moment and relegate them to a lifetime of punishment and stigma. We tell ourselves the lie that now we are safe.

To be clear, I believe in accountability for crimes, but after forty years toiling in the world of courts and jails, I can tell you one thing with certainty: we don't hold people accountable; we destroy them. Those who rehabilitate do so despite our harsh sentences and conditions of confinement, not because of them.

We must somehow find the courage to face our fears. I'm not asking you to push them away. We are hardwired to be fearful. I'm simply inviting you to lean toward fear, sit with it, be curious, and question it.

In most areas of our lives, we try to rationally assess risk to manage our emotional response. We know that car accidents happen, but we drive to work anyway because the odds are that it won't happen to us. Planes crash, but we fly because a crash is the outlier, not the norm. We read warning labels on medications that tell us all about the risks of terrible reactions, but we swallow the pill anyway because we want to feel better, and we understand the side effects are unlikely. All of us assess risk regularly and recognize that sometimes bad things will happen. But we take these risks because the immediate tangible benefit is "worth the risk."

One of the challenges of criminal justice reform, which is unlike a flight or most medicines, is that there is no immediate tangible benefit. But that doesn't make the reform less critical. We invest in education. We invest in health. We invest in our children. None of which demonstrates immediate tangible results in the short term, but all of which reveal huge long-term benefits from our effort and our patience. Learning to control our fear is worth the risk and can have tremendous impact on how we treat one another.

I was recently reminded of how hard it is to be courageous when you are scared. Late one night, I was alone, asleep in my bed, when I heard noises coming from the back of my house. A couple days earlier, someone had broken into our garage and stolen a bicycle, so I was on high alert. Concerned that someone might come into my house if I didn't jump into action quickly, I crept quietly down the stairs in my gray flannel robe, with bare feet, and headed toward the noise. I was scared. I had no idea what was waiting for me on the other side, but I took a breath, unlocked the door, and slowly pushed it open.

I was startled to see, not more than three feet from me, a tall, stocky man with bloodshot eyes and a brightly colored headband covering his forehead. Our eyes locked and I tried to quickly assess him. "What are you doing?" I asked firmly but softly. "Can I help you with something?"

I had no idea what would happen next, but I checked my emotions and stayed in the present. "What's happening here?" I asked with genuine curiosity.

"I'm just looking for something to sleep on. See? There's cardboard. I don't know why no one likes me. Why does no one like me? No one likes me," he mumbled.

His vulnerability hit me. I could feel the fear beginning to leave my body. "I don't feel that way," I said. "Just take what you need from there. It's okay. And stay safe tonight." With that, he turned his attention from me back to the recycling bin, removed more of the cardboard sheets that were inside, and quickly walked away into the night.

I closed the door and went into the kitchen to make some tea, hoping it would help me get back to sleep. Later in bed, both dogs by my side, I replayed the scene in my head. On the one hand, I felt good about the result. I didn't call the police, so they weren't needlessly deployed and he didn't wind up in jail, arrested for stealing cardboard. I didn't bring my two pit bulls downstairs to terrify him. I never even raised my voice to threaten him, even though I might have been within my rights to do so.

Instead, I assessed the situation and him as carefully as I could, not ignoring my fear but rationally managing it. I engaged with this stranger rather than allow my imagination to fill the void with worst-case scenarios. I chose to be curious. Instead of fear, I felt a profound sadness as I replayed his words in my head. I wondered who he was, who he had been, and what might become of him.

I know that some of you are thinking that I just got lucky, that the man could just as easily have been a "psycho killer" looking for his next victim (though, really, what are the statistical odds of that?). Others might think I'm just naive or a bleeding heart with no common sense at all. Neither is true.

What you now know from this book is that my perspective has been shaped by a lifetime working in the criminal justice system with the very people we are taught to fear. The stories we tell ourselves, believing we are keeping ourselves safe, can become self-fulfilling prophesies. Had I come down the stairs screaming and threatening with a weapon in my hand, who knows what might have happened. Of course, I also get scared sometimes, but curiosity remains my ally, along with a deep belief that we are all better than the worst thing we've ever done.

Reason can keep abstract fear at bay, but only curiosity can build a bridge to understanding when we fear one another.

Curiosity opens a window into the world of another person, past what we project or think we know about them. Curiosity opens us up to the reality of someone else's experience—someone who may look nothing like us and whose life seems far away from ours. Curiosity opens us up to one another's suffering and reveals the rich shared ground of our common humanity underneath.

Curiosity is also the precondition for something equally important. Without it, we will never be able to change our systems or how we see one another. Curiosity is the precondition for compassion, and the courage we need to tame fear. If we are ever to evolve our notion of justice, it will take more than the courage of conviction. It will take the courage of compassion.

"So what?" some of you may be asking yourselves. After all, you probably didn't sign up for criminal justice reform. You aren't obligated to advocate for people who are accused of crime, so what relevance does it have to you? Why should you care?

Criminal justice reflects a history and power structure, but it also mirrors how we come into society and show up for one another. We live in a time when we easily reduce one another to our political stances, leaving no room for nuance or our larger stories. We "cancel" people out of existence with no possibility of a way back into a community. Our imagination turns those who disagree with us into caricatures that we can easily hate, dismiss, and dehumanize. We've never been more knowledge-able yet less curious about others and why they might think the way they do.

What if it turned out that developing the curiosity and com-passion of good public defenders enabled us to move closer to one another? What if that perspective helped us hear one another better, even when we disagree? What if it helped us scream less and understand others more?

Perhaps the next time you find yourself in the middle of a contentious political debate, you can open your mind, listen more, and try to understand how your opponent arrived at their point of view. Or the next time you see a mug shot on the front page of your local newspaper or flashed across the television screen, withhold your judgment and be curious about the human being behind the red, tired eyes. It's not easy, but it's possible. It is the courage of compassion in action.

This is what public defenders try to do every day. I'm not suggesting you become a public defender and battle it out in court every day, but I am suggesting that if we learn to develop the same sensibility in life, it will help us become better, happier, and less afraid human beings with the capacity to build a stronger and greater society.

12

The Courage
of Compassion

If you had told me years ago that I would write a book about discovering compassion, I would have told you that you don't know me. I would have written you off. Scoffed at you like I scoffed at the woman who told me I'd trade in my sharp elbows, black boots, and East Coast edge for "cleansing breaths" after living in LA for a year. Not a chance.

Certitude certainly has its drawbacks.

For decades I have been speaking out about the injustices I've seen in America's criminal courts. And I have been seeking the answer to one question: What will it take to make this system more just, more humane?

I thought the answer might be revolutionizing public defense, bringing class action lawsuits, or organizing with clients. Or maybe the solution was to focus on a single issue, like women's mass incarceration or ending cash bail. I built organizations, led trainings, and stood in front of countless auditoriums, lecture halls, and television cameras describing the often-unseen brutality of our justice system and demanding change.

To be sure, working from within the system taught me important lessons about what it takes to challenge entrenched interests. But it was the day-in-and-day-out relationships with the people I represented that did more to swell my heart with urgency and deepen my thinking about what is needed if we are ever going to create better justice practices.

It has taken me more years than I care to admit to understand that America's criminal justice system isn't just a manifestation of "the powers that be" but also a reflection of our own fears, indifference, and lack of mutual understanding. To know what happens inside the criminal justice system and take responsibility for the role *we all* play in it is to confront uncomfortable truths about ourselves. As Nelson Mandela once said, "no one truly knows a nation until one has been inside its jails."[1]

As a society, we have never been more technologically connected, yet Americans express feeling increasingly alone, alienated, and misunderstood. According to a recent survey, more than three in five people in the United States report feeling lonely.[2] Anxiety and social isolation brought on by the COVID-19 pandemic made matters worse, but the conditions for our growing feelings of separateness existed long before.

We crave genuine connection, but all too often we lack the genuine compassion necessary to forge these connections.

Looking back, I realize that serving as a public defender gave me more than I ever gave. Encompassing all of it was a feeling of belonging and connection to others: of being part of a shared human struggle, a community not of identity but of hope and compassion for one another.

Compassion is a unique form of human connection that is transformational. It opens us up to the suffering of another as if it were our own. It compels us to act. Understanding how systems perpetuate racist outcomes and economic inequality can help us draft better policies, but only the inner work of compassion can give us the courage to change ourselves and thus what we expect from justice. Compassion restores our shared humanity. Indeed, it gives us back ourselves, freer and more authentic. It's a magical thing to witness, especially when it goes both ways.

My husband, David, once represented a man named Trey. They were around the same age.

Trey was charged with an armed robbery, an allegation he steadfastly denied. It was what we in public defender circles call a "one-witness ID" case, where the only evidence against the accused is a single witness who claims to be able to identify the person who committed the crime. That's it. That's the whole case.

There was no physical evidence, no confession, and no video to indicate that Trey was the person who committed the robbery. The victim had picked Trey's picture out of an array of photos shown to him by the local police. Later, he had picked him out of a police lineup conducted hours after he pointed to Trey's photo and stated that he thought Trey was "the guy."

I can't count the number of times I have watched a television show and heard a victim say of the perpetrator: "I'll never forget that face." It may sound like it makes sense—after all, wouldn't you remember the person who robbed you?—but science and years of research have proved otherwise. It is actually incredibly hard to get it right, especially when identifying someone of another race.

Here, the prosecution's case relied solely on a cross-racial identification by the victim, who had only frantic and terrified minutes, in the evening hours, to see the person who robbed him.

David, who was never one to leave a single stone unturned in defense of a client, had also become our resident expert on identification procedures and their inherent unreliability. He even brought novel legal motions challenging the way that the NYPD conducted identification procedures and rigorously conducted pretrial hearings on the matter. He was the perfect defender for Trey. So when the judge who was assigned to oversee Trey's case told David that he was "fully familiar with the vagueries" of cross-racial identification and the unreliability of one-witness-identification cases, David thought the judge was giving him "the wink." Encouraged by the judge's statements and knowing that jurors often have a hard time grasping the science of misidentification, David advised Trey that their best strategy was to waive a jury trial and try the case to the judge.

Trusting David's instincts, Trey agreed to waive a jury and the trial began.

David tried the case with all the brilliance and tenacity I had come to appreciate about him over the years. He presented the scientific literature, calling into the question the legitimacy of the identification procedure, and cross-examined the witnesses pointedly. At the close of the case, I sat in the front row and watched the perfectly crafted summation.

"Will the defendant please rise," the judge said the next day, having given himself the night to think about his verdict. Trey and David stood up. "I find the defendant guilty." I could hear David's gasp from where I was sitting in the audience. I could not see Trey's expression, just his shoulders rising as he took a deep breath. The judge rattled on about how much he "appreciated" the concerns about cross-racial identification procedures and how unreliable they might be.

Then he sentenced Trey to fifteen years in prison.

David left public defense a few years after the trial. I have always wondered if Trey's trial propelled his departure from public defense. At first he stayed in touch with Trey, but after a few years they stopped writing. I knew that David carried with him the guilt of Trey's conviction, so when David moved to California to begin a career as a TV writer, it came as no surprise that he was driven to tell human stories that broke the *Law & Order* mold and exposed the cruelty of the criminal justice system.

Many years later, while I was still running the Bronx Defenders, I got a phone call from Trey, who was now out of prison. I was delighted to hear his voice. I told him that David had moved to California and was writing for TV. Trey loved the idea of David as a television writer and asked me to send him his best. "I can do better than that. Why don't I arrange for you two to see each other when David's in town?" I said. "I know he would like to see you."

The morning of their meeting, I was surprised to see David walk into my office at the Bronx Defenders with a collared shirt on (he always wears flannel) and real shoes, not his usual sneakers. Clearly, he had dressed up for the meeting. As we sat on the sofa in my glass-walled office, looking out at all the public defenders hard at work on the floor, I could see that David was uncharacteristically nervous. Since he was someone who almost never exhibited anxiety of any kind, I knew this was a reckoning of sorts for him. Before I could ask him about it, Trey walked into my office. He flashed a big smile and without missing a beat threw his arms wide and shouted: "Dave!" David didn't hesitate. They embraced, holding each other tightly, until they both sat down, side by side.

"You look good, Dave. You put on a little weight, I see," Trey teased. David patted his belly and laughed. I looked across the room at these two men, who were now almost identical in size, height, and girth, and thought back on that day—more than a decade ago—and all that had happened in between.

"So how you been, Dave?" Trey asked. David began to answer, but before he could get more than a few words out, his voice broke, his brow knotted, and I could see that he was fighting back tears. Trey leaned toward David. "Dave, what's wrong?" he asked, looking concerned. Trey tried to catch his gaze, but

David just kept looking down and shaking his head. "I'm sorry, Trey. I'm so sorry. I never should have waived a jury. I never should have trusted that fucking judge. I know better. I'm so sorry," David choked out. Trey looked over at me. I could see that he was bewildered by David's reaction, so I just nodded, affirming the pain he was witnessing. Trey leaned over, getting so close to David that their heads were almost touching.

"Dave, you've been carrying that all these years?" he said, putting his hand on David's shoulder. "Don't do this to yourself, man. I'm all right."

David finally looked up at him. "How can you be all right? It was so wrong, so fucked up, and I let it happen to you," David said.

Trey sat up in his chair, shook his head, and continued, "Dave, listen to me. I spent years in prison next to guys who ate themselves up every day over the what-ifs. *What if* I had a good lawyer? *What if* someone had actually fought for me? *What if* my lawyer had cared? Those guys, for them, the time was really hard to do. They ate themselves up. It wasn't like that for me. Come on . . . Dave . . . I'm a Black man. I know what the system does to us. I know how it operates. I never expected anything different. But I never ever, not for one second in all those years in prison, said 'what if.' Never. 'Cause you fought for me; you gave it everything you had. I never doubted that. I'm grateful for that. Dave, you must let go. Stop worrying about me and something that you had no control over. I'm good. See? Look at me," he said, leaning back in his chair and patting his belly. "I'm really good."

I could see David take in Trey's words. In that moment they

were no longer lawyer and client. They were just two men connected to each other by mutual compassion.

As I close the final chapter of my career, the biggest lesson I can offer is perhaps the simplest. Not the easiest, but the simplest: be curious, get proximate to the suffering of another, and have courage.

Reimagining justice as something more than retribution is possible.

It starts with each of us.

It starts when we finally see ourselves in the faces of those ensnared in our criminal justice system and when we see our children in their children.

It starts when we allow ourselves to feel another's pain as our own.

It starts with compassion.

It is in that deepest of places that you discover love as a political force, and you can't help but muster the will to want to change the world.

Now close this book, shut your eyes, and take one of those long, cleansing breaths . . .

A Letter to a Young Public Defender

So here you are. Law school is done. You have done the internships. You survived the bar exam. Now, to the dismay of your parents, you are choosing to be a public defender instead of vying for a job at a fancy law firm or clerking for a judge.

Congratulations.

I have many regrets, but becoming a public defender was never one of them. Doing this work was never a sacrifice. It gave me a higher purpose. It gave me the sorts of friendships and love that form only in the midst of battle. It taught me that there is always more to a person than meets the eye. It showed me that if you want to change the world, the most radical thing you can do is extend a hand—and I don't mean just metaphorically—to the one who's marginalized, shunned, or demonized.

It is a life's calling if there was ever one. But I won't lie to you. It is not glamorous work. Far from it. And if you think you know exhaustion and heartache, prepare yourself for a whole new kind of despair. I'm really selling it, aren't I? Well, the truth is that if you decided to become a public defender, you must have thought long and hard about *why*. Clearly, it wasn't for the money or the status. It was something else. Something deep inside you that said, *I can't look away*. But there will be moments when you forget. It happens to all of us, even the most militant and politically committed. So I'm here to share three ways in which I always found the way back to my core purpose in choosing this path, in the hope that someday they might be useful to you too.

I would say three traits define most public defenders. They definitely applied to me—for better and for worse. Each can offer you an insight into yourself and a shortcut to that place where you can see clearly why you get up each day to fight for a perfect stranger.

The first: You love and have loved deeply flawed individuals, perhaps to your own detriment. But it has taught you that a person is complex, beautiful, and always unfinished. It has taught you that we are the sum of our stories and that new stories can always be written. It has taught you that you don't have to forget in order to forgive. It has taught you that love is stronger than disgust, fear, and hate. Can you love a perfect stranger? You can, but it takes courage, because love implicates you in another's life, and with that comes responsibility. When you love, you can't ignore suffering. You need to do what you can to make it right. To others, you will say you do this work because you believe in justice, due process, and the adversarial system. But the fuel that really keeps you going is that you end up caring deeply for the people entrusted to your defense. I encourage you to see your work as an act of love. It will keep you constantly redefining what we even mean by that word, but it will only make you stronger. I promise.

Second: You have a healthy dose of mistrust for authority. Perhaps you grew up without a source of legitimate authority in your life. Perhaps whatever authority there was soon revealed its arbitrary nature and darker side. One thing is true: you believe authority must be earned and re-earned on a daily basis. The first day you walked into an arraignment, your eyes opened to what passes for justice in this country. And you saw the people in power and you wondered how in the world they were ever entrusted with such authority over life and liberty. You also began to see the entire machine and realized injustice is more complex than bad policies. And you promised yourself that even though you were becoming "an officer of the court," you would never become a cog in the machine.

There will be days when you feel like a cog. It's inevitable.

There will be days when you will realize how your mere presence as the "defense function" can add a veneer of legitimacy to the indefensible. And you will wonder if you should rebel against it. Quit out of principle! Move to a policy organization so you can make "real" systemic change. Three words: Check. Your. Ego. Look at the case file in front of you and remind yourself that behind that number there's an entire life. Here's the thing. A machine can't function without cogs, but a machine begins to break only when enough cogs go off-kilter. Opting out may make you feel good about yourself, but it leaves those ensnared in it alone, undefended, and vulnerable. The machine is going to come for your client. Your role is to make sure it must go through you first.

Third: Like me, you were once probably idealistic about change. You were ready for the revolution. You thought, *If I shout loud enough, things will change.* They won't. You will simply become annoying, then marginalized, and ultimately ignored. Injustice in America is bigger than any one policy, any one party, and any one institution. But here you are. No longer reading the books that will change the world but wearing a court-ready suit and carrying a briefcase. You wonder: *What the hell happened to me?* Well, at some point you realized that injustice is not something abstract. It is something that is rained upon individuals, families, and communities. And you decided to do something about it.

This is it. And while it won't change the world tomorrow, the client you represent means the world to someone today, and that is a world that is fully in your care now.

This book is titled *The Courage of Compassion* because all those times I thought I had lost my ability to keep on fighting, I rediscovered my courage through the strength and resilience of the people whom I had the duty and honor to defend. Law school doesn't teach you much. But it does teach you a bit of Latin. The word *compassion* comes from Latin. It has two parts. *Pati*, which means *to suffer*. And *com-*, which means *with*. Compassion is to suffer with another. It is not to pity them. It is not to have mercy for them. It is to be *in it* with them, arm in arm. And this is how we affirm our common humanity. This is how you fight for a perfect stranger whose dignity is under attack, as if your own life depended on it. Compassion is the key to action. Without it, nothing will change.

Open your heart and focus your mind. The struggle for social justice is long and winding, but it is won one person at a time.

Onward.

ACKNOWLEDGMENTS

I never in my wildest dreams thought that I would write a book. Really. It seemed too daunting, too intellectual, and maybe even a little self-indulgent. But here I am . . .

The experience of creating this book has been magical. Not just because I got to spend every day with Camilo, my coauthor, (although that was clearly part of it) but because it gave me the opportunity to reflect on my career and the people who helped me get to today.

At my age, there are so many people who have influenced and nurtured me along the way. I can't name you all—I only hope that I did a sufficient job at the time of letting you know how much I valued you. But some special mentions are in order.

Acknowledgments

I owe so much to the countless people whom I have had the privilege of standing with as their public defender over the course of my career. Thank you for your wisdom, for your resilience, and for trusting me with your stories. I have learned more from you than words can capture.

Thank you, Camilo Ramirez, my coauthor, colleague, and friend, for your brilliance, kindness, dedication, and creativity. This book is as much yours as it is mine, and I never could have done it without you. Thank you for being chosen family, along with Nina, Alma, and Max, and for our adventures together. Your courage of compassion is at the very heart of this book.

It is undeniable that family influences who we become. We tend to remember their failings more than the gifts they gave, but I am grateful for all of it. Thank you to my father, who taught me how to love flawed people, and my mother, who taught me what resilience looks like. Thank you to my brother, Robert. I have loved you from the moment they brought you home. We rose together, baby brother. And to my grandparents, Jerry & Bert and Anna & Peter, for modeling what it means to fight for a cause you care about and without whom I simply wouldn't have made it.

For me, creating new organizations is a lot like raising children—you pour your heart into them, and then, one day, it is time for them to go out into the world without you. It's hard, but knowing that they will be nurtured by other extraordinary caregivers makes letting go possible. Thank you to the incredible Bail Project team, especially Kaitlin Koga and David Gaspar, whose brilliant leadership at the Bail Project made it possible for me to step away. I am forever grateful to you both. And thank you to Justine Olderman and Aisha McWeay for graciously leading the Bronx Defenders and Still She Rises into being the impactful public defender offices they are today.

For me, knowing whom I can count on and who will show up for me matters deeply. People come and go, but my lifeboat is reserved for those I know I can trust with everything. First and foremost, thank you to my BFF for the last fifty years, Mitchell Klein—from our rebellious teenage years to our alte kaker beach walks, we are in this together, forever. To Earl Ward, Abbe Smith, and Seann Patrick Riley for always bravely showing up, no matter what, and to Susan Elbe, Laurie Barron, Carol Rosenthal, and Bobbie Spellman for your love and decades of friendship.

Doing this work has never felt like a sacrifice, but I am keenly aware that those around me made many sacrifices that made my career possible. Thank you, Fred, for supporting and encouraging me through my journey from Legal Aid to the Bronx Defenders and for our most precious children.

Thank you to my incredible children, Jacob and Emma, for all those times growing up when you understood and selflessly pushed me out the door saying: "Mom, just go. . . . Your client needs you now." I love you unendingly and am so proud of you both—for being the remarkable humans that you are, for caring about justice, and for showing compassion. Being your mother is the greatest gift of all.

Thank you to every staff member over all the years—from

the amazing young assistants to the brilliant senior staff at the Bail Project, Still She Rises, the Bronx Defenders, Neighborhood Defender Service of Harlem—who focused on those we serve first, while working tirelessly to build these organizations and make a better world.

Thank you to the many supporters and funders who believed in the work of the Bail Project, Still She Rises, and the Bronx Defenders. It takes courage to support bold ideas and put your resources, and reputations, on the line because you believe in justice. Special thanks to: George Kaiser Family Foundation, especially the brilliant Amy Santee for her guidance and friendship; TED and Chris Anderson for believing in the Bail Project and taking away my notes and glasses; the Audacious Project, especially Anna Verghese and Danielle Thomson, who saw the promise of scaling the Bronx Freedom Fund and made it happen; Mike Novogratz for his audacious generosity and his willingness to get proximate; Blue Meridian Partners for their world-changing investment in the Bail Project, especially Mindy Tarlow, whose thought partnership has been indispensable; the board of directors of the Bail Project for their faith in me and for helping steer the ship through the clear and choppy waters; Bridgespan Group, especially Rohit Menezes and Sridhar Prasad, who brought their intelligence to this Bail Project journey from the very beginning.

Thank you to everyone at Penguin Random House for convincing me that I had something to say. Thank you Adrian Zackheim, Niki Papadopoulos, and especially Kimberly Meilun for your smart editorial comments. A big special thanks to Simon

Sinek for your impactful encouragement—your insights, passion for new ideas, and belief in the possible made this book so much better. I'm proud to be part of Optimism Press.

And finally, thanks to my partner in crime and life—my husband, David Feige. It's been a long and winding road. From working side by side with you as young public defenders to marrying you in that old, abandoned courthouse in the South Bronx, under the chuppah in a sandbox we built, I love you and am so grateful to and for you. Thank you for always wanting to slay every dragon for me and for loving me no matter what. I know I don't always make it easy, but without you, I would not be who I am. So until the very end of my days on this earth . . . come find me.

Get Involved

Freedom Should Be Free

Fixing America's criminal justice system appears insurmountable at times. People often ask me: "What can I do? Where do I start?" Tactically speaking, there is no better place to start than working to reform the cash bail system.

While we might disagree on the larger questions of law enforcement, prosecution, and sentencing, one thing should be indisputable: money has no place in a true justice system. The right to be presumed innocent. The right to due process. These treasured constitutional protections that are at the heart of American democracy should never come with a price tag.

Since 2017, the Bail Project has been working to take money out of the justice system. The Bail Project provides free bail assistance to thousands of low-income Americans every year, along with support for returning to court and connections to social services and community resources. Through these efforts, the Bail Project gathers human stories that illustrate the urgency of bail reform, as well as evidence to prove that cash bail is not needed to ensure people come back to court.

To learn more about these efforts and get involved, visit bailproject.org.

NOTES

Chapter 1: How Can You Defend "Those People"?

1. Helen Fair and Roy Walmsley, "World Prison Population List," 13th ed., World Prison Brief, 2021, prisonstudies.org/sites/default/files/resources/downloads /world_prison_population_list_13th_edition.pdf.

2. Alexi Jones and Wendy Sawyer, "Arrest, Release, Repeat: How Police and Jails Are Misused to Respond to Social Problems," Prison Policy Initiative, August 2019, prisonpolicy.org/reports/repeatarrests.html.

3. Brian Elderbroom et al., "Every Second: The Impact of the Incarceration Crisis on America's Families," FWD.us, 2018, everysecond.fwd.us/downloads /everysecond.fwd.us.pdf; Matthew Friedman, "Just Facts: As Many Americans Have Criminal Records as College Diplomas," Brennan Center for Justice, November 17, 2015, brennancenter.org/our-work/analysis-opinion/just-facts -many-americans-have-criminal-records-college-diplomas.

4. Léon Digard and Elizabeth Swavola, "Justice Denied: The Harmful and Lasting Effects of Pretrial Detention," Vera Institute of Justice, April 2019, vera .org/downloads/publications/Justice-Denied-Evidence-Brief.pdf.

5. Jacob Whiton, "In Too Many American Communities, Mass Incarceration Has Become a Jobs Program," Brookings Institution, June 18, 2020, brookings.edu /blog/the-avenue/2020/06/18/in-too-many-american-communities-mass -incarceration-has-become-a-jobs-program.

6. Wendy Sawyer and Peter Wagner, "Mass Incarceration: The Whole Pie 2022," Prison Policy Initiative, March 14, 2022, prisonpolicy.org/reports/pie2022 .html; "Fast Facts on U.S. Hospitals, 2022," American Hospital Association, 2022, aha.org/statistics/fast-facts-us-hospitals.

7. Elizabeth Hinton, LeShae Henderson, and Cindy Reed, "An Unjust Burden: The Disparate Treatment of Black Americans in the Criminal Justice System," Vera Institute of Justice, May 2018, vera.org/downloads/publications/for-the -record-unjust-burden-racial-disparities.pdf.

8. Scarlett Lewis, "Kindness Can Be Taught. Here's How" (interview by Cory Turner and Anya Kamenetz), NPR, May 13, 2019, npr.org/2019/05/09 /721721668/kindness-can-be-taught-heres-how.

Chapter 3: Fighting For versus Fighting Alongside

1. Sol Wachtler, "A Jurist's Prudence: A Q&A with Sol Wachtler" (interview by Morgan Pehme), City & State New York, December 17, 2014, cityandstateny .com/politics/2014/12/a-jurists-prudence-a-qa-with-sol-wachtler/179705.

2. New York State Association of Criminal Defense Lawyers and National Association of Criminal Defense Lawyers, "The New York State Trial Penalty: The Constitutional Right to Trial under Attack," 2021, nysacdl.org/page /NYTrialPenalty21.

3. Benjamin Weiser, "Trial by Jury, a Hallowed American Right, Is Vanishing," *New York Times*, August 7, 2016.

Chapter 4: Throwing Stones versus Befriending the King

1. Simon Sinek, conversation with the author, May 2022.

Chapter 5: Defeat versus Resilience

1. The Innocence Project, "Report: Guilty Pleas on the Rise, Criminal Trials on the Decline," August 7, 2018, innocenceproject.org/guilty-pleas-on-the-rise -criminal-trials-on-the-decline.

2. Saul M. Kassin et al., "Police-Induced Confessions: Risk Factors and Recommendations," *Law & Human Behavior* 34 (2010): 5, web.williams.edu/Psychology /Faculty/Kassin/files/White%20Paper%20-%20LHB%20(2010).pdf.

Chapter 6: Knowing It versus Feeling It

1. "National Inventory of Collateral Consequences of Conviction: An Online Database Cataloguing all 40,000-Plus Collateral Consequences in the U.S," Council of State Governments Justice Center, accessed June 3, 2022, csgjus ticecenter.org/publications/the-national-inventory-of-collateral-consequences -of-conviction.

2. Alexi Jones and Wendy Sawyer, "Arrest, Release, Repeat: How Police and Jails Are Misused to Respond to Social Problems," Prison Policy Initiative, August 2019, prisonpolicy.org/reports/repeatarrests.html.

3. Equal Justice Initiative, "America's Massive Misdemeanor System Deepens Inequality," January 9, 2019, eji.org/news/americas-massive-misdemeanor-system -deepens-inequality.

4. Matthew Friedman, "Just Facts: As Many Americans Have Criminal Records as College Diplomas," Brennan Center for Justice, November 17, 2015, brennancenter.org/our-work/analysis-opinion/just-facts-many-americans -have-criminal-records-college-diplomas.

5. The Sentencing Project, "Report to the United Nations on Racial Disparities in the U.S. Criminal Justice System," April 19, 2018, sentencingproject.org /publications/un-report-on-racial-disparities.

6. Foster Kramer, "The Poorest Congressional District in America? Right Here, in New York City," *Village Voice*, September 30, 2010, villagevoice.com/2010 /09/30/the-poorest-congressional-district-in-america-right-here-in-new-york -city.

7. Robin Steinberg, "Heeding Gideon's Call in the Twenty-First Century:

Holistic Defense and the New Public Defense Paradigm," *Washington & Lee Law Review* 70, no. 2 (2013): 960–1018, scholarlycommons.law.wlu.edu/wlulr /vol70/iss2/6.

Chapter 7: Judgment versus Curiosity

1. U.S. Census Bureau, "America's Families and Living Arrangements: 2021," table FG10, census.gov/data/tables/2021/demo/families/cps-2021.html.

Chapter 8: Comfort Zone versus Uncomfortable Truths

1. Inimai M. Chettiar, "The Hidden Bearers of Mass Incarceration: Women," Brennan Center for Justice, July 18, 2017, brennancenter.org/our-work/analysis -opinion/hidden-bearers-mass-incarceration-women.

2. Elizabeth Winkler, "Why Oklahoma Has the Most Women per Capita in Prison," *Wall Street Journal*, January 2, 2018, wsj.com/articles/why-oklahoma -has-the-most-women-per-capita-in-prison-1514898001.

3. Wendy Sawyer and Wanda Bertram, "Prisons and Jails Will Separate Millions of Mothers from Their Children in 2022," Prison Policy Initiative, May 4, 2022, prisonpolicy.org/blog/2022/05/04/mothers_day.

4. Aleks Kajstura, "Women's Mass Incarceration: The Whole Pie 2019," Prison Policy Initiative, October 29, 2019, prisonpolicy.org/reports/pie2019women .html.

5. Rebecca Shlafer et al., "Children with Incarcerated Parents—Considering Children's Outcomes in the Context of Complex Family Experiences," University of Minnesota Extension, Children, Youth & Family Consortium, June 2013, conservancy.umn.edu/handle/11299/151818.

6. "Grounds for Involuntary Termination of Parental Rights," Child Welfare Information Gateway and U.S. Department of Health and Human Services, Administration for Children and Families, Children's Bureau, 2021, childwelfare .gov/pubpdfs/groundtermin.pdf.

7. Andrea J. Sedlak et al., "Fourth National Incidence Study of Child Abuse and Neglect (NIS-4): 2009–2010," U.S. Department of Health and Human Services, Administration for Children and Families, Office of Planning, Re-

search, and Evaluation and the Children's Bureau, 2010, cap.law.harvard.edu
/wp-content/uploads/2015/07/sedlaknis.pdf.

8. Susan George et al., "Incarcerated Women, Their Children, and the Nexus with
Foster Care," National Institute of Justice, April 2011, ojp.gov/ncjrs/virtual
-library/abstracts/incarcerated-women-their-children-and-nexus-foster-care.

Chapter 10: Skin in the Game versus a Pound of Flesh

1. Alain Sherter, "Nearly 40% of Americans can't cover a surprise $400 expense,"
CBS News, May 23, 2019, cbsnews.com/news/nearly-40-of-americans-cant
-cover-a-surprise-400-expense.

2. Testimony by Attorney General Robert F. Kennedy on Bail Legislation, Before
the Subcommittees on Constitutional Rights and Improvements in Judicial
Machinery of the Senate Judiciary Committee, 88th Cong., 2nd sess. (1964)
(statement of Robert F. Kennedy, U.S. Attorney General), justice.gov/sites
/default/files/ag/legacy/2011/01/20/08-04-1964.pdf.

3. "The Civil Rights Implications of Cash Bail" (briefing report, briefing before
the U.S. Commission on Civil Rights, Washington, DC, January 2022), usccr
.gov/files/2022-01/USCCR-Bail-Reform-Report-01-20-22.pdf.

4. "Civil Rights Implications of Cash Bail."

5. United States v. Salerno, 481 U.S. 739 (1987), supreme.justia.com/cases/federal
/us/481/739.

6. "Pretrial Justice: How Much Does It Cost?" Pretrial Justice Institute, 2017,
s3.documentcloud.org/documents/3439051/Pretrial-Justice-How-Much
-Does-it-Cost.pdf.

7. Jennifer L. Doleac, "New Evidence That Access to Health Care Reduces Crime,"
Brookings Institution, January 3, 2018, brookings.edu/blog/up-front/2018
/01/03/new-evidence-that-access-to-health-care-reduces-crime.

8. Wendy Sawyer, "How Race Impacts Who Is Detained Pretrial," Prison Policy
Initiative, October 9, 2019, prisonpolicy.org/blog/2019/10/09/pretrial_race.

9. H. Mitchell Caldwell, "Coercive Plea Bargaining: The Unrecognized Scourge
of the Justice System," *Catholic University Law Review* 61, no. 1 (Fall 2011): 63–96,
scholarship.law.edu/cgi/viewcontent.cgi?article=1003&context=lawreview.

10. Robin Steinberg, Lillian Kalish, and Ezra Ritchin, "Freedom Should Be Free:

A Brief History of Bail Funds in the United States," *UCLA Criminal Justice Law Review* 2, no. 1 (2018): 79–95, escholarship.org/content/qt37s1d3c2/qt37s1d3c2 .pdf.

Chapter 11: Fear versus Courage

1. Megan Brenan, "Worry about Crime in U.S. at Highest Level Since 2016," Gallup, April 7, 2022, news.gallup.com/poll/391610/worry-crime-highest-level -2016.aspx.
2. Holmes Lybrand and Tara Subramaniam, "Fact-Checking Claims Bail Reform Is Driving Increase in Violent Crime," CNN, July 7, 2021, cnn.com/2021/07 /07/politics/bail-reform-violent-crime-fact-check/index.html.
3. German Lopez, "Examining the Spike in Murders," *New York Times*, January 18, 2022, nytimes.com/2022/01/18/briefing/crime-surge-homicides-us.html.
4. "Car Crash Deaths and Rates," National Safety Council Injury Facts, accessed May 20, 2022, injuryfacts.nsc.org/motor-vehicle/historical-fatality-trends /deaths-and-rates.
5. "Drug Overdose Death Rates," National Center for Drug Abuse Statistics, accessed May 20, 2022, drugabusestatistics.org/drug-overdose-deaths.
6. Beth Schwartzapfel and Bill Keller, "Willie Horton Revisited," The Marshall Project, May 13, 2015, themarshallproject.org/2015/05/13/willie-horton -revisited.
7. Alexi Jones and Wendy Sawyer, "Arrest, Release, Repeat: How Police and Jails Are Misused to Respond to Social Problems," Prison Policy Initiative, August 2019, prisonpolicy.org/reports/repeatarrests.html.

Chapter 12: The Courage of Compassion

1. Nelson Mandela, *Long Walk to Freedom* (Boston: Back Bay Books, 1995), p. 201.
2. Elena Renken, "Most Americans Are Lonely, and Our Workplace Culture May Not Be Helping," NPR, January 23, 2020, npr.org/sections/health-shots /2020/01/23/798676465/most-americans-are-lonely-and-our-workplace -culture-may-not-be-helping.

INDEX

Index

Index

Index

Index

Vernon Correctional
  Center, 30
Veterans Affairs (VA), 154

Wachtler, Sol, 26
war on drugs, 6
Weinstein, Harvey, 174–75
what-ifs, 207

women, incarceration of, 4–5, 145,
  147–48, 202
Women's Prison Project, 4, 53
women's rights, 50

X-rays, 110, 115, 116–18

Yom Kippur, 122, 123–24